GOING MY WAY

A FINANCIAL ADVISOR'S REFLECTIONS ON LIFE

SAMUEL M. DENNY

PRAUSPRESS

DEDICATION

To my parents, Waller Sam and Pat Denny,
who took the time to invest in me.

And to my wife Linda,
who has been the best investment decision I ever made.

ACKNOWLEDGEMENTS

Special thanks to Byron Crawford for his encouragement and support
while this book was in its formative stages; more importantly,
for the kindness he has shown my family over a period of years.

A word of thanks to Adrian Layne, friend and client,
who provided able assistance in reviewing the final draft of this book.
The insights provided were invaluable in helping
to determine the direction of the final text.

A heartfelt thanks to my financial services clients past
and present for allowing me to be a part of their lives both
personally and professionally.

TABLE OF CONTENTS

FOREWORD

If you think you may be picking up just another nuts-and-bolts book about how to manage your money, you are in for a surprise. In this fascinating collection of short stories, Sam Denny makes silk purses from the change of piggy banks with thoughtful reflections upon many lessons from his personal life that became cornerstones of his successful financial counseling career. These include such intriguing story titles as, "About the Lone Ranger, Silver Bullets and the Secret Silver Mine," "Walt Disney's Snow White and the American Work Ethic, "Too High and Right Down the Middle," "And Bring Me Back the Change."

In these stories and many others, Sam relates interesting, amusing and often poignant, remembrances from real life to saving and investing. You may finish this book so captivated by the warmth, wit and wisdom of its stories that you forget you have also just read a series of great tips for financial success.

Sam learned his craft from one of the best—his father, the late Waller Sam Denny, who was an accountant, a great storyteller, a fine man, and a true friend of mine over the many years when I was the Kentucky Columnist for the *Louisville Courier-Journal*. Although his father is gone, I hear his voice in Sam's writings, and can glimpse a few priceless moments when his father and his wonderful mother, Pat, were shaping Sam's judgment with practical lessons that he has never forgotten. In these pages, you will discover that they work as well for daily living as for financial serenity.

Sam, since your father is not here to tell you this, please permit me the privilege of saying it for him: "Good work."

Byron Crawford
Columnist, *Kentucky Living Magazine*

SAMUEL M. DENNY

CHOOSING A FINANCIAL ADVISOR FOR LIFE

If I were to ask you today who advises you on financial issues, you may or may not mention folks who do so for a living. Perhaps prior to choosing your advisor, you sought out references as to their abilities and most importantly, their character.

I was fortunate that when I chose my first financial advisor, I did so based on a strong character reference from my pastor at the time. My choice was the choice of a lifetime. I was three days old when I made it. What follows is the reference letter my pastor sent to me dated June 15, 1951 ...

My dear little friend,

Your advent into this earth came at a very busy time for me, and I wish to apologize for being so tardy in getting over to see you. But yesterday I was able to see your fine mother for a few moments, and a kind nurse let me have a fleeting glimpse of you.

There are many things that I want to tell you, but because you are not able to bear them all now, I'll try to keep the number of subjects which I shall discuss small. First of all, I want to congratulate you for your choice of parents. You see, they love each other very much—so much in fact, that they wanted some little angel to share that love with them. I am so happy that you noticed that love, and decided that you wanted to share in it. As you grow older and wiser, you will notice that love is the most remarkable power in the world.

I am also happy that you decided to be a boy. I know that your father is already planning a noble life of baseball, fishing, and long walks through the woods with you. He will make you a fine partner. Your mother also has great hopes and dreams for you, because every mother wants to be proud of her son.

Now one other thing, and I am through. You are coming into a pretty rough old world. We old folks have become very confused in our thinking. We have forgotten that

our Lord told us to be as a little child. But more than that, we have forgotten that we
are children of our heavenly Father. Dear lad, never become so big that you forget that.
I hope we shall become great friends in the future.
Your pastor and friend, Harold M. Parker, Jr.

At three days of age, I chose my parents as my financial advisors. My father, who worked as an accountant, believed in teaching the fundamentals, whether it was finances or sports. He was careful with money, in part to care for the family and in part to be generous toward others. My mother was not financially sophisticated but was financially competent; after my father's death, she used that knowledge to help the Hispanic community in our hometown of Louisville, Kentucky. They worked as a team throughout their marriage of 47 ½ years, at times having to change their roles due to illness and the permanent loss of my father's job at the age of 40 due to disability. Over time, they steadily built a comfortable retirement for themselves and later for my mother as a widow. While they may have not had advanced training in finance, they understood the basics concerning money. What they understood the best was that having a healthy relationship with your financial resources is better than simply having the largest portfolio.

If you are raising children (and perhaps even if you are not), you are someone's chief financial advisor. That young person will look to you for direction and ultimately copy many of your behaviors, both financially and in other areas of life. That responsibility is awesome and at times overwhelming, and as my pastor pointed out indirectly, perhaps the greatest gift you can give your children is to have as many good people in their lives as possible. Dear parent, never become so distracted that you forget that.

THE VALUE
OF TEAMWORK

When I was 12 years old and my brother was 9, my father coached our Little League baseball team. I treasure that experience if for no other reason, it was the only organized activity that all three of us were able to participate in together. Our team, which was made up of mostly nine-year-olds in a league of nine-to-twelve-year-olds, started the season with a dismal record of two wins and six losses. About that time my father took the team aside and told us the following:

"Guys, we're at a point where we can start fresh. If we keep hustling, never quit, and pick each other up, there is no telling how things will turn out."

The remainder of the season was an almost magical experience. Our team won 10 games in a row and finished the season as the best team in the league. All of us had taken to heart what my father had said and the effort had more than paid off. What I did not realize at the time was that in order for our team to be successful, my father as coach had to continually make adjustments until he found a winning combination. And when he found that winning formula, out of the nine positions on the field, only two of us were playing the same position at the end of the year that we had been playing at the beginning. As adults, we also are searching for that winning combination both in our personal lives and in our financial lives. At times, we also may look to a fresh start and may need members of our team— whether parents, teachers, coaches, or those we do business with—to play different positions for our team to be successful.

Just as in sports, both in our business lives and in our personal lives, it takes a variety of skills to create a successful team. The most successful businesses need both creative ideas and responsible money management—dependable employees as well as leaders. The most successful relationships are those where each individual is aware of and respects the talents and skills of the other person.

When my wife and I were first married, we faced the challenge that both of us had financial backgrounds and were used to making our own financial decisions. Over time, we learned that our family functioned best with my wife being the manager and distributor of financial resources, while I was best suited to being the preserver of the resources we had. This allowed both of us to "play within ourselves." Our family as a whole functioned better knowing that my wife and I were clear as to our roles in handling our money. Yet had circumstances required us to do so, each of us could have "come off the bench" and played the other's role in our family's financial life.

As adults, we need to provide opportunities for our young people to learn the importance of teamwork in relationships and in financial decisions. Perhaps one day there will be youth sports camps that focus less on teaching individual skills and more on teaching the team concept. Perhaps as parents we can involve our children in an age-appropriate way concerning family financial decisions. Most of all, we need to fully understand the role we are best suited to play in order for our families to thrive. For as my father encouraged and advised our Little League baseball team years ago:

"keep hustling, never quit, and pick each other up."

SAMUEL M. DENNY

THE TALE OF UNCLE REMUS

As a small boy growing up during the 1950's, I was exposed to the Uncle Remus animal stories both in written form and when watching the 1946 Walt Disney movie "Song of the South." Like most children of that time, I was entertained by the adventures of Brer Rabbit, Brer Fox, and Brer Bear. As an adult, I in turn read a number of the Uncle Remus stories to my two children as they were growing up during the 1980's. However, as time passed the Uncle Remus stories have fallen into disfavor in that the setting of the book serves as a reminder of the wrongs in America prior to the Civil War. Going forward, it remains important to remove as many signs of racial inequality as possible. Yet in a way we have lost sight of a number of messages and opportunities that the Uncle Remus legacy offers to us.

It is worth noting that the setting in which the Uncle Remus stories were told centered around the strong friendship of a young boy (who was white) and an older man (who was African-American). The boy looked up to the older man and treasured the stories that the older man shared with him. Unknown to the boy he was also being taught through the stories character traits that he would find useful in later life. In return, the presence of the young boy brought joy and meaning to the older man's life. Both young boy and older man felt free to give and receive in friendship.

I recall my father telling me that my uncle had a similar friendship with an older African-American man while growing up in the small town of Lancaster, KY during the 1920's. And like in the Uncle Remus stories, my uncle treasured the time he spent with the older man. The relationship continued even after my uncle became a career navy officer stationed in various parts of the world. Whenever my uncle would return to Lancaster, he made it a point to look up his old friend and reconnect with him. I remember my uncle being described as a "southern gentleman" in the purest sense of the word. I cannot help but think that the influence of his older friend helped mold him into the man he became.

GOING MY WAY

Over my lifetime, I've worked as a volunteer at several schools in the Jefferson County (KY) public school system. During that time, I served as a mentor to several African-American boys. While with most of the boys the relationship ended when the school year ended, with one young man the relationship has continued to the present. LeRoy was 10 when I first met him in his fifth-grade class in the fall of 1993. I remember asking him, "LeRoy, how are you doing?" LeRoy's response was "Mr. Denny, how are YOU doing?" I couldn't help but marvel at LeRoy's ability to bypass the social barriers people often put up and in so doing, create opportunities for meaningful communication. LeRoy soon wanted to know if I was open to him calling me at work or at home. From there we had a number of phone conversations about a wide variety of topics.

As LeRoy grew older, the phone conversations became fewer, but we were still able to maintain contact and during Christmas season in 2018, I received a call from LeRoy wishing me a good holiday and asking "Mr. Denny, how are you doing?"

I told LeRoy that I was doing fine. This time his response was "Oh, come on. You've got to have a hangnail or have stubbed your toe. How are you REALLY doing?"

LeRoy told me about his school-aged daughter and shared with me the hopes he had for her future. He told me that my presence in his life had given him a more positive view of white people than he would have had otherwise. And at the end of our phone visit, he told me that he loved me. I left our conversation both humbled and with a sense of fulfillment. I also realized that I have a lot to live up to going forward.

On my desk at home there is a picture taken 25 years ago that I treasure to this day. In the photo, I am standing with two boys and have an arm around each one of them. One boy is my son who now works as a city attorney. The other boy is LeRoy. The picture is a reminder for me of how open and caring communication can help in overcoming differences between people. And I also find myself reminded of times in my life where simple things—an old bubble-gum football card, a peanut butter and jelly sandwich, or rolling a ball with a preschool aged boy — broke down barriers of race and socioeconomic status. Going forward may we all work to model for our young people an understanding and appreciation as to the life's journeys of others.

SAMUEL M. DENNY

THE EASTER EGG HUNT (HOW TO TEACH A PRESCHOOLER THE VALUE OF SAVING FOR THE FUTURE)

For many of us in this country, Easter is one of the most joyous and most meaningful holidays of the year. Families attend church together, eat a meal afterwards, and often settle in to watch the children participate in an Easter egg hunt. These plastic eggs are filled with candy of some sort; there is an air of excitement as the children search and claim their treasure.

My triplet grandchildren are no exception. At three years of age, they eagerly anticipate the opportunity to search for the hidden eggs, then enjoy the rewards of their efforts. They are also in an age-appropriate way getting a lesson in the importance of working toward a reward however short-term the reward happened to be. So what if we as adults could take the egg-hunting activity and turn it into a lesson on the concept of saving money? Let's try this idea on for size.

On a more regular basis than once a year, perhaps a small child can go on a search for plastic eggs. As opposed to putting candy inside the eggs, put pennies in the eggs instead. For eggs that are relatively easy to find, put one penny in. For eggs more difficult to locate, put more than one penny inside. Once the child had found and opened the eggs, he can count the pennies and put the total amount into a large glass jar that allows him to see all the pennies he has collected. At the point that the jar becomes full or too heavy to lift, we can tell him that we are going to take the pennies to a place (a bank or credit union branch office) where they will take care of his pennies for him. It would also be wise to together count the pennies and put them into wrappers prior to going to the bank.

We can also tell him that he may be given something (probably a sucker) for letting the bank take care of his money. Later in life he will learn about the concept of interest, but for now the immediate reward of a sucker can serve as "interest" on his money

As a child grows older, we can build on the concept of the work involved in obtaining money and give the opportunity to handle nickels, dimes, quarters, and dollars as well as pennies. While this may require extra effort on the part of the adults, hopefully the reward for all of us will be a young person who recognizes that it takes more than a "swipe of the card" to obtain the things you want in life.

ROOM 632—
BAPTIST EAST HOSPITAL

During the spring of 2015, I began to have medical distress symptoms that persisted and worsened. After about a week, my wife took me to a hospital emergency room early on a Sunday morning. Upon examination, I was admitted and within hours, medical personnel were addressing my condition. I was told that pending test results, I had a rare intestinal disorder that would require surgery. In the interim my stomach was being pumped in preparation for the procedure. While I had spent a number of hours in hospitals as a caregiver for loved ones, this was the first time I had ever been admitted myself. What lay ahead was a life's learning experience both for me and for my family.

As a patient in the hospital, my standing in the world suddenly changed. I no longer had anything in my possession that gave me identity. The clothing I had been wearing, my wallet, and my car keys were now in my wife's care. Being confined in the hospital rendered me largely unable to take care of my day-to-day duties as the owner of a small insurance office. Though in a good marriage with a caring and devoted woman, I was now living in one world and she in another. As I lay in the hospital room, I looked for the emotional resources needed to make a proper adjustment.

I then remembered how I had felt when I had left home to begin my freshman year of college. Just as I had adjusted to a life change at the age of 18, I could try to do the same during the course of my hospital stay. And so I began to navigate my situation knowing it could be a time for learning and personal growth.

I got to know the nurses, aides, and custodial personnel who were providing my care. What particularly interested me was the depth of many conversations. With one nurse conversation revolved around my experience of having in-laws provide day care for children. With a second it revolved around spiritual beliefs and how a profession can also be a calling to help others. With a third it centered around ways to help her and her husband better communicate as to their financial decision making. For even though I was a patient in a hospital I found myself in a position to provide care towards those who were caring for me. I hope that I was as empathetic towards them as each of them was towards me.

My surgery was successful and I was discharged after a stay of six days. Within the week, I had returned to work part-time and was fully integrated into life at home. Yet there was still one piece of unfinished business and that was how to properly thank everyone who had cared for me. So about two weeks after my discharge I bought two pies at a local bakery and took them to the nurse's station. Upon my arrival, I was greeted by the nurse who had confided in me as to her financial issues. She told me that I looked good, then hugged me and said, "Thank you! What you shared with me has gotten my husband and me talking more. Things are so much better!" I thanked her and told her I hoped things would continue to go well. From there after talking to several other staff members I returned home.

Hopefully a stay in the hospital for any of us does not occur any time soon. And yet there is no better time than now for each of us to be thankful for the care we receive from others on a day-to-day basis. Sometimes the care is of a physical nature. Sometimes the care is emotional support. More often than we realize, the care can be of a financial nature. The opportunities of providing care occur often and sometimes unexpectedly. For as one of the nurses at the hospital said to me while struggling to get some monitoring equipment to work properly, "Lord, give me patience!" My response to her (in jest) was this — "Kara, you have five patients, including me."

SAMUEL M. DENNY

ABOUT THE LONE RANGER, SILVER BULLETS, AND THE SECRET SILVER MINE

As a boy growing up, my favorite television program was (and still is) "The Lone Ranger," which aired originally during the 1950's and remains available via reruns and in DVD box sets. The show helped me develop an appreciation for classical music – in addition to the introduction from the William Tell Overture, the background music for the episodes included excerpts from the work of classical composers such as Beethoven, Schubert, Wagner, Mendelssohn, and Weber.

The masked ranger rode throughout the West with his Indian friend Tonto, righting wrong wherever he saw it, then vanishing just as mysteriously as he had arrived. His trademark silver bullets were obtained from a "secret silver mine" that also was the source of income to meet his everyday needs.

As a longtime viewer of Lone Ranger episodes, I gradually became aware that the Lone Ranger made use of the silver bullets available to him in two ways. When a confrontation with one of the "bad guys" was unavoidable, the Lone Ranger fired a silver bullet from his gun with the intent of shooting the gun out of his opponent's hand. The Lone Ranger never shot to kill, but only to hold his opponent fully accountable for inappropriate behavior. At other times after making a bad situation right again, the Lone Ranger would then hand a silver bullet to the person he had just aided. The silver bullet was a symbol of the values that the Lone Ranger stood for, yet also could be used to help the recipient with any financial issues they might have had.

In our relationships with those people we care about, especially while we are raising our children, it appears to me that at times we find the need to use "silver bullets" as well. If our children are doing something that we know to be unhealthy or wrong, we may have to fire the silver bullets of discipline and accountability in order to get them back on the right path. At other times, the silver bullets may take the form of a gift. The gift make be in a tangible form such as providing for a child's college education. Or the gift may simply consist of being available to provide emotional support and instilling a set of values that will serve our children well as adults. Either way, it is at times an awesome and overwhelming responsibility to make sure that we use our silver bullets wisely.

In the end, as children grow into adulthood they will discover the location of the "secret silver mine." Knowing the location of the mine will hopefully enable our children to refine the silver ore (the values and standards needed to lead an honorable life) and in turn pass silver bullets on to their children. From there we can ride off into the sunset just as the Lone Ranger and Tonto often did. Yet as we ride off, we will leave our loved ones with the assurance that just like the Lone Ranger, we will always be back if we are needed.

MISSING PERSONS FILE
(MARCH 1999)

Over the years, I've had the pleasure and privilege of being a part of several high school reunion committees. As the planning process for each reunion progressed, committee members took on roles best suited to both their interests and capabilities. In my case, the role of locating missing members of the class became my task. Many of the classmates I have located over the years were found prior to the rise of social media. Perhaps the most enjoyable experience I had when locating a missing classmate centered around someone I had not been in contact with for 30 years.

Greg Stairs was my teammate in a couple of sports. We played on the same Senior Little League baseball team for a few seasons, with his father being one of the coaches. We also were on the same team playing in a weekend pickup basketball league. As such, I was surprised when in the spring of 1999, Greg Stairs turned up on the missing classmates list. I had no idea where Greg was living, but I remembered that Greg's family had moved to New Jersey a couple of years after graduation. After learning what town the family had moved to, I called directory assistance in New Jersey asking for a listing on Greg's father. I was told by the operator that there was no listing for Greg's father but that there was a listing for an "S. Stairs." Recalling that Greg had a younger sister named Susan, I asked for the listing and took a shot in the dark by calling the number.

To my surprise (and I suspect far more to Susan's surprise), I found myself in touch with someone who could help me reach Greg. I explained my reason for calling, then added I would end the call should it become uncomfortable for her. Susan graciously agreed to talk with me during what turned out to be a pleasant 30-minute conversation. I found Susan's demeanor over the phone especially refreshing in that it conveyed a calm and soothing presence, while at the same time retaining the youthfulness of the cheerleader she had once been. At the end of our conversation, Susan passed on to me Greg's contact information. I then thanked her for the information and for the enjoyable conversation we had.

From there, I left a couple of messages for Greg by phone. One evening, about six weeks after I had talked with Susan, I received a call from Greg. The voice on the other end of the phone was upbeat and conveyed a zest for life that radiated throughout. Over the course of an hour, Greg and I traded notes about our high school years and where we had journeyed since then. Greg was in attendance at our 30-year reunion. As with our phone conversation, I was able to enjoy his company in person. As Greg put it to me later "I made the reunion AND I HAD A BLAST!"

It strikes me as interesting that as more means of communication have become available, there seems to be less actual direct communication between people. Were I trying to locate Greg Stairs today, I simply could check nationwide phone listings via the internet and discover that there are but two listings for Greg Stairs in the entire country. Or perhaps I could have utilized Facebook, Twitter, Google, or any other number of social media sites.

However, I would have never had the opportunity to enjoy first the refreshingly soothing conversation with Greg's sister, nor later the upbeat and engaging personality of Greg himself. So, the next time any of us may want to reach an old friend, perhaps the more traditional means of communication—a handwritten letter, a phone call, a personal visit—may turn out to be more rewarding for both you and the person you are reaching out to. All the best to each of you as you continue to connect with those who have been a part of your life's journey.

SAMUEL M. DENNY

" ...AND BRING ME BACK THE CHANGE"

When I was in early grade school, I tended to do two things that concerned my parents: one was to miss the school bus on a regular basis (which eventually was addressed in a quiet yet decisive manner) while the other was to lose the quarter which I was given daily to pay for lunch at school. Concerned about my lack of financial responsibility, my parents — and my father in particular — searched for a way to make me more aware of the importance and value of money. How my father instructed me to be financially aware I have never forgotten. What follows is the setting where the lesson was taught.

On the occasions when our family went out to eat, we dined at the old Kaelin's restaurant located about a mile or two from our home in Louisville, Kentucky. At that time Kaelin's was unique in two ways. First, Kaelin's is recognized as the place where the cheeseburger was first created. Second, it was one of only two restaurants in the world that served Kentucky Fried Chicken.

When we sat down for our meal, a waiter dressed in a white coat and black bow tie took our order, brought our food out to us, then presented us with the bill to be paid at the end of the meal. My father would take me aside and show me the bill, asking me to check the addition to see if it was correct. I was then given the bill, along with the necessary money, and instructed to go to the register to pay the bill. If the bill was added incorrectly, it was up to me to point out the error prior to giving money to the cashier. My father had also taken the time to help me determine how much change, if any, was due back. His final instructions were what told me that I was fully responsible for the transaction being completed correctly, "—and bring me back the change."

GOING MY WAY

How many times have we as adults handed our young people money for a transaction and not asked for the change? While we may believe that we are being generous with them, we are also depriving them of the opportunity to experience being held fully accountable for the handling of money. So the next time you take your family out to eat at a sit-down restaurant — the Cracker Barrel being a favorite of mine where a family of four can eat for under $50— keep one of the menus after you order. Go over with your son or daughter what had been ordered and determine how much it will cost. Factor in a tip if the service has been good (while my father was always open to tipping the restaurant staff, he did not consider tips an entitlement). When the meal is over, send your son or daughter to the register with a $50 bill and have them pay the tab. Imagine how they will feel being entrusted with what to them is a large sum of money. And just as my father did years before, say to them as their last instruction "—and bring me back the change."

SAMUEL M. DENNY

WALT DISNEY'S "SNOW WHITE" AND THE AMERICAN WORK ETHIC

When my daughter was preschool age, she was taken to see the Walt Disney movie "Snow White." First released in 1937, the movie was the vehicle that brought Walt Disney into national prominence. In the movie, Snow White was helped by seven dwarfs who befriended and cared for her. Ultimately, she was rescued by a handsome prince and whisked away to live "happily ever after." The movie made an impression on my daughter. More than once when we were out as a family, she would make us wait for her to help seven imaginary dwarfs get their coats on and follow us to the car before we could return home. Perhaps the two most memorable songs in the movie were "Someday My Prince Will Come" and the work song as sung by the seven dwarfs. And like most young girls, whether they have seen the "Snow White" movie or not, my daughter looked forward to the day when her prince would come.

The intervening years passed by quickly. My daughter is now a grown woman. She married, but did not marry into a family of royal blood. She is the mother of two young children—my grandchildren—who are loved but will never ascend to a throne. Instead of a castle, she now resides in a comfortable home that comes complete with a monthly mortgage payment. And in order to help make sure that she and her family live happily ever after she has held a job as a project manager for a major corporation. The song in the "Snow White" movie that she relates to most now perhaps is different from the one she related to as a small child. That song is the one sung by the seven dwarfs and also sung by millions of Americans — with a slight change in the wording — while on their way to their place of employment:

"I owe, I owe, so off to work I go . . .
I owe, I owe . . .
I owe, I owe, so off to work I go . . .
I owe, I owe . . ."

I leave it to you to figure out the remaining verses (and ultimate outcome) of the song.

AN AFTERNOON WITH "THE GREATEST"

During the summer of 2009, I had opportunity to tour the recently opened Muhammed Ali Museum. Also along for the tour was my grandson Johnny, who at the time was only eleven months old. As a lifelong resident of Louisville, Kentucky I had followed the life of Muhammed Ali as he evolved from heavyweight boxer into perhaps the most recognized personality in the world. Visiting the museum was an opportunity to gain additional perspective into Ali's unique and remarkable life.

As we toured the museum we saw countless news stories about Ali on display. We read a story written the day after he first won the heavyweight boxing title from Sonny Liston. We read about his decision to embrace the Muslim faith. We perused stories about his decision not to enter military service and the subsequent fallout that resulted both nationally and for Ali personally. And we read about Ali regaining his boxing title and becoming an internationally renowned personality.

Yet there was another aspect of the Ali story that we would get to experience. For on this summer afternoon we were about to meet "The Greatest" in person. While we were on the third floor of the museum, a fellow visitor had indicated that he thought Muhammed Ali was on the premises. Within five minutes, we encountered Ali in the company of his wife, Loni Ali, and his sister-in-law. They were headed to the museum theater on the second floor where visitors could watch film of his various title fights. Upon meeting us, Loni extended an invitation to accompany them to the theater. Surprised and pleased by the invitation, we and approximately a dozen other visitors followed the Ali family to the theater.

As we walked to the theater, I was struck by a number of things I observed as to Muhammed Ali. At 67 years of age he was limited in his movements by Parkinson's disease, yet at the same time he still had the forearms of a young man. Though his face seemed to have a blank look, his eyes were actively taking in what was going on around him. There was no entourage — he was accompanied only by his family and I found it ironic that while as a young man he communicated through bravado in a violent sport, as an older man he was communicating a message of inclusiveness simply by his presence and persona. Words were not needed. For while the body of Muhammed Ali may have been weakened, it was also allowing his strength of spirit to shine through.

At the theater, Ali sat in a lounge chair and watched film from his 1966 title fight with Cleveland Williams as one of the other visitors providing commentary. At the same time, my grandson Johnny was at the nearby scale size boxing ring pulling himself up on the ropes and scooting himself around. While Ali was interested in the fight film, I could also see his eyes intently watching Johnny as he traveled along the ropes, as this was a man who was known for his love of children. After the film concluded, an opportunity was extended for Johnny to have his picture taken with Muhammed Ali. Though the photo that was taken did not come out as clearly as we would have liked, it was still on record that during the summer of 2009 my grandson Johnny had spent an afternoon with "The Greatest."

Fast forward to the spring of 2016 and my grandson Johnny is a first-grade student at a Louisville public school. He has been given the class assignment of making a poster about a famous American. It goes without saying which famous American he picked. Included on the poster is a copy of the picture taken with Muhammed Ali when Johnny was but eleven months old. The caption beside the photo simply reads like this:

"Float like a butterfly, sting like a bee"

Picture of Johnny, with Muhammed Ali

THE WISDOM OF A FATHER

Not long ago, I received a phone message at my insurance office from Frank Polion, one of my longtime clients. Years before I had helped Frank and his wife, Annita, start a college savings program for their two children. As their daughter was planning to attend college in the near future, Frank had requested that I meet with him and both of their children to review the accounts. I was not completely sure what I would be asked to share with the family. Yet as our meeting began, I realized that my presence was to affirm the wisdom of a father—a father who had instructed his children as to the value of education in a way that I had not witnessed before.

As his children listened attentively, Frank Polion spoke as to how he felt a college education was meant to utilize a person's talents and gifts and mold them in a way that would make that person a productive and self-supporting member of society. At the same time, Frank took the opportunity to affirm with his children the special gifts he felt each of them had to offer. He stressed that paying for a college experience was a team effort— done not just with a savings program, but also with scholarship money and part-time work income the children could earn. Yet most importantly, Frank emphasized that while he and Annita had been saving for their children's college, they were also providing for their own future so as to not become a financial burden on their children. After Frank finished speaking, he deferred to me. I readied myself to answer any questions the Polion children might have.

Both daughter Danielle and son Josh asked a number of well-thought-out questions as to what the college savings program provided for them and about college life itself. Most of what I shared with them centered around both the joys and pitfalls of day-to-day college life, reinforcing what their father had taken time to share with them. Yet perhaps the best question came from Josh toward the end of our meeting. He asked a question that people of all ages ask, "How do you go about networking for your future?"

I was initially unsure as to how to answer Josh and told him as much. What I did share with him were a couple of instances as to how I had re-connected with people after a long period of time. One centered around an old bubble-gum football card that had special value to the family of the player depicted on the card. The other centered around how after nearly 50 years I had a unique opportunity to thank a fellow student from my high school years—a person who had patiently taken the time to tutor me in a challenging course. I then asked Josh if I had answered his question. He responded, "Absolutely!"

The value of higher education is communicated regularly to our young people. Yet it seems all too often that it is conveyed in the narrow context of future career options. All of us—myself included—can learn from parents such as the Polions. For if more parents realize that prepar-ing for higher education is a continual and broadly based process, more young people will find fulfillment in life and find it sooner.

ABOUT SIBLING RIVALRY

Like most siblings, my brother Jim and I periodically had our differences while growing up. I don't know if it began when he kept knocking over my building blocks or when I pushed his stroller into a clump of sticker bushes. But as we became adults, I thought we had put our issues behind us. So it surprised me, when in our 50's, Jim began to refer to me as an "old dude." I became even more concerned when I learned he had described me as a "numbers freak" to a group of mutual friends.

"Freak?" What had I done to deserve this? I now knew that there was but one thing to do. That was to call our mother and ask her how to resolve our issues. And there was one tool I knew I could use to get Mom's full attention—that was to use our childhood names as I presented my case.

"Mom," I began. "This is little Hammy Morgan. Little Jamie Hud keeps calling me names!"

"Well, what names did he call you?" Mom asked.

"HE CALLED ME AN OLD DUDE!"

Mom tried to comfort me, yet brought a degree of reality to the situation. "Son, you know you are older than your brother and that you always will be older than he is. There really isn't anything that we can do about that."

"I guess you're right," I said. "But you know what else he called me?"

"What was that?"

"HE CALLED ME A NUMBERS FREAK! AND HE DID IT EX-ACTLY THREE TIMES!"

Mom was now more concerned than before. "Don't you think you are getting a bit anal about this?"

"Well, it's just not fair!" I answered. "I don't know what to do!"

Mom sat quietly and began to draw on her years of experience for a possible solution. After a short time, she offered me this plan of action:

"Call him one back."

During the last year of our mother's life, she was told by her doctor that she was no longer capable of living by herself. So with the help of his wife Annie, my brother Jim provided round-the-clock care for Mom. He managed her medications, prepared her meals, served as her contact person with medical personnel, and throughout gave of himself to her out of love. So regardless of whatever names Jim chooses to call me in the future, it is now time to call him names back just as our mother had instructed me. Names such as "caring." Names such as "compassionate." Names such as "honorable." And it was Jim who gave our mother the ultimate validation when he commented on the four open-heart surgeries she had survived. He told her in front of a large group gathered to celebrate her 80th birthday "the doctors may say Mom has a bad heart, but we all know she has a perfect heart."

As we live our lives going forward, I would like to offer some things each of you might want to put on a wish list. To start, mothers (and fathers) who have perfect hearts. Siblings who we can call names — such as caring, compassionate, and honorable. Friends who enrich our lives simply by their presence. Finally, a sense of meaning and fulfillment in all aspects of your life. May all of these gifts be passed on to you and yours for the taking.

"JUST SAY NO"

During my children's elementary school years, they participated in a program for drug awareness education offered by their school. The program was taught by local police officers and included role-playing, workbook assignments, and a ceremony to recognize completion of the program. A central focus of the drug awareness program was to instruct students to "just say no" when drugs were offered. Yet while the program appeared to be well-structured and taught in an open and caring manner, it seemed to me that there was but a mixed level of success as the students got older.

Peer pressure certainly plays a role in the lives of young people, often making it difficult for them to "say no" to potentially self-destructive situations. Yet there seems to be another factor that influences how young people handle peer pressure; that is how their parents and other significant role models "say no" to situations in their lives. My wife and I participated in a family focus group for several years and it intrigues me that one of the major issues all of the members were working on was how to "set boundaries" in a healthy manner. How many of us as adults after deciding to say "no" then try to explain our decision to the other person and in turn set ourselves up for a debate in the process? As such, I wonder if we are really trying to convince ourselves more so than the other person.

Over the long term, it appears that the best way to teach a young person how to "say no" is simply by the example we set. Saying no is not just about drugs or alcohol, but also spoken to handling our finances in an irresponsible manner. If our children see us as content with the home we live in, the cars we are driving, the style of clothes we wear, and the social contacts we have, then implied permission has been granted for them to do the same. And when we or our children have to "say no" in a particular situation, our reasons boil down to simply the way we have patterned our lives on a day-to-day basis, which does not necessarily require a verbal explanation.

SAMUEL M. DENNY

AND WHO IS MY NEIGHBOR?

On a cold winter day in 1982, I was driving home with my daughter, who was only one year old at the time. En route home, the car ran out of gas as a result of what I learned later was a leaking gas tank. Stranded at the bottom of a steep hill on a busy four-lane highway, I got my daughter out of the car and carried her to the top of the hill where a small gas station was located. I obtained a gallon gas can, filled it with gasoline, and we returned to the car. Strapping my daughter back into her car seat, I put gas in the tank and completed the trip home. As this event occurred prior to the rise of cell phones, my options were limited and I was relieved to have both myself and my daughter home safely.

The following Sunday, our family attended our home church as we did regularly. After the service, various members greeted others and exchanged the usual pleasantries. Included in this group was an older couple who had known both my wife and me since we were preschoolers growing up in the church. After the standard greeting and handshake from both of them, the woman added, "Oh, by the way — we saw you carrying your daughter on the road last week." I did not give the comment further thought, but when I shared it with my wife, she asked me a simple but direct question — "Why didn't they stop to help you?"

The question hit me at the core of my being. This older couple had seen both my wife and me grow up in the church, meet and become married there, work with church youth and in church government, and most recently become parents of a young daughter. The couple regularly ate with my parents after church services. They went out of their way on many occasions to help others, particularly my father who was permanently disabled. By all accounts, they were honorable people.

Yet for some reason I did not warrant the same attention that my parents and others received. And if I was unable to depend on this couple, who I had known in church most of my life, who in a church setting could I depend on?

That Sunday was the last time I set foot in my home church as a member. I did not attend any church for about a year. Eventually my wife and I began attending another church, but it was many years before I could begin to trust the intentions of anyone within a church setting. I have largely come to terms as to the hurt I felt when the older couple left me on the highway in an hour of need. Yet to this day I still tend to question the sincerity and intent of greetings I may encounter after a church service.

It seems that today our society is bombarded by messages from a number of worthwhile organizations who ask for our time and/or our financial support. Yet I wonder if these messages desensitize us as to need in our own back yard. This past fall I noticed that my neighbor across the street was constantly having to rake up large numbers of leaves that did not come from his property. Aged 70 and with a heart condition, he eventually ran out of energy in early January and left a large pile of leaves in his yard for weeks. Noting that, I went to his home to bag the remaining leaves for him and carry them out to be recycled. That day my neighbor was an African-American man named George Wallace, as opposed to a charity requesting donations. Who is YOUR neighbor TODAY?

THE PARABLE OF THE TALENTS—FOR TODAY

As one who attended church on a regular basis, I have been present during a number of financial stewardship campaigns to raise the money for the work of the church. The pastor more often than not will base his message on the "Parable of the Talents" found in the New Testament of the Bible. In the story, a man who is leaving on a faraway journey entrusts his financial resources to three "stewards." Upon his return, he asks the stewards to account for the status of his money. Two of the stewards had grown the money significantly and were praised and rewarded for their efforts. The third steward had buried the money entrusted to him and was penalized because he had done so. The story is about the prudent use of our personal abilities as well as our financial assets. What interests me about the story is that there is no mention as to how the first two stewards went about growing the money entrusted to them.

Given the times in which we live, perhaps the story of the "talents" might take a different direction if told strictly in a financial context.

A man who worked for a large international corporation was called in by his supervisor and told he was being transferred to a job overseas that would last for a period of five years. Prior to leaving he met with three financial professionals and hired them to manage his money. To one he entrusted $50,000. To the second he entrusted $20,000. The third was given $10,000 to manage. Upon his return the man called in each professional in order to review his accounts. The first professional who had been given $50,000 to manage now had but $40,000 remaining. Upon being questioned as to the losses the response was "the market will come back in time. We'll just have to ride it out."

The second professional who had been entrusted with $20,000 was called in. He had but $15,000 remaining of what he had been entrusted to manage. Upon being questioned he too responded, "the market will come back in time. We'll just have to ride it out."

The third professional was called in. Upon being questioned he responded, "I knew it was important to you that your account grow, but also I felt it was best that it grow in a stable and predictable manner. Your money was put in a guaranteed rate of interest for the five-year time period. Your account has grown from $10,000 to $11,500.

I leave it to you as an individual to write your own ending to the story.

SAMUEL M. DENNY

BABY STEPS TO
FINANCIAL SUCCESS

Recently my wife and I, who up to now had just one grandchild, became grandparents to four additional children within a period of six months. We have watched with pleasure as each of the babies have reached important milestones in their development. We have noted when each of them was able to hold his or her head up, turn over without help, sit up unaided, crawl, and eventually walk steadily. And we will witness additional developmental landmarks as each child starts to feed themselves, acquires language, becomes "potty trained," and receives their first experiences in structured learning settings.

It goes without saying that the parents are excitedly keeping close tabs both as to developmental milestones reached by their children and looking to developmental skills yet to be mastered. And if the parents of these young children could use the same developmental milestones in establishing a long-term financial blueprint for their family, wouldn't it be at least worth a look?

Anyone who has raised or is raising small children is aware that there are three continual expenses for a new, growing family. The first can be the cost of formula and/or strained food. The second is the cost of diapers. The third is the cost of day care. So what would happen if when these three expenses are reduced or eliminated, the family would simply commit that same amount of money towards a long-term savings program? The savings program would be started when the child is fully integrated into table food (around the age of one). Upon the child being "potty trained" (around the age of three) take the amount that is no longer being spent on diapers and increase contributions to the account. Finally, when the child reaches school age take the amount saved on day care and again increase account contributions.

Making these three investments could result in hundreds of dollars per month being put back for the long-term future of the entire family. The end result could be less (if any) college debt for children and/or a sizable nest egg for the parents.

All of us have been made aware of the need to set aside money for the future both for ourselves and our families. But too often the message that is being sent is more about WHERE money should be allocated and not WHEN are the most opportune times to take steps towards saving for the long term. The first baby step, or course, is putting a plan into effect. For as I was once told "It is never too early — and never too late — to begin saving for the future."

SAMUEL M. DENNY

SAVING VERSUS INVESTING
(A DIFFERENT PERSPECTIVE)

Recently the pastor of my church led our Sunday School class in a study of the Protestant Reformation. Over a six-week period, my wife and I learned about the efforts of Martin Luther and other clergy to institute changes in some of the practices of the Roman Catholic church. One of the changes that occurred was the elimination of the concept of purgatory. Purgatory was defined by the early church as the soul entering a state of suspended animation (neither heaven nor hell) when a person died. To supposedly get a loved one from purgatory to heaven, the church collected a predetermined amount of money that was called an indulgence. While this practice allowed the Roman Catholic church to build large cathedrals and supply a comfortable standard of living for church officials, it was not a guarantee as to a person's afterlife.

While the concept of purgatory is no longer a part of religious life in this country, it seems that in the last century we in the United States have created a kind of social purgatory that we refer to as adolescence. Our young people find themselves living in a state of suspended animation from their teens into their mid-20's, not being fully recognized as adult until about the age of 25 (if not beyond). Just as during the Middle Ages, parents are looking for a way to get their son or daughter out of such a state of flux. The way out chosen by many families is paying out a predetermined amount of money to guarantee that a young person will be able to enter the adult world. The money is paid to a standing social institution, but that institution turns out to be colleges and universities, as opposed to the early church. And the document that is given out today has a different name that it had in the Middle Ages. It is referred to as a diploma in today's society.

Both in the Middle Ages and in today's society, people were looking for a way to save their loved ones and were willing to pay large amounts of money to guarantee the result. Yet the money spent was in reality an investment and did not necessarily guarantee the outcome desired. When it comes to our relationships, we are always investing in others in the hopes of the healthiest outcome for all concerned. Had I realized this earlier in life, I would have been a better parent to my children and a better husband to my wife. In the financial world saving is possible and can take a number of forms (even under the mattress) that can lead to a predictable outcome. Investing whether with money or in relationships should be entered into with a willingness to accept an outcome different than what was first expected. For knowing when to save and when to invest — whether with our financial or our emotional resources — is a key in finding fulfillment in all aspects of life.

SAMUEL M. DENNY

ACADEMICALLY INELIGIBLE

For the better part of 25 years I served as a volunteer youth soccer coach at the local YMCA, working with children ages 4 and 5 every fall and spring. My longest tenured player was a boy named Jeremy, who played for a total of five seasons. I enjoyed my time being Jeremy's coach. By nature, he was cooperative, friendly, and as one parent put it was going to do "something" while on the playing field. Jeremy also improved steadily as a player and by his fourth season, he was enjoying success and scoring goals regularly. So, when in the middle of that season I was told by his parents that he was going to be held out of soccer due to significant misbehavior at school, I was caught completely off guard. Regardless, as coach I supported the decision to put Jeremy on the "academically ineligible" list.

Jeremy was held out of practices and games for a week's time. From there his parents decided to let him play again…but not without reservations. The behavior issues, though improved a bit, had not been resolved completely. At that point, I asked his parents if I could get involved as I knew the principal at his school and would be willing to talk to her. Jeremy's parents liked the suggestion and told me it was OK to move forward. So on the Monday following his most recent game, I gave the principal a call.

I related to her my experience in working with Jeremy over the prior four seasons. I noted that he had always been cooperative and fully engaged in a sport that was continuously moving and active. The principal now had a picture of Jeremy that was dramatically different from what was being reported to her at school. She indicated she would look further into things and asked me to give her a rundown of his last soccer game. Our conversation ended with the principal simply saying "leave the rest to me."

The principal spent one-on-one time with Jeremy and gave him a rundown of his last game as I had described it to her. As I was told later "his eyes got real wide" when she congratulated him on the three goals he had scored in the game. After spending the time with Jeremy, the principal determined that he would thrive in settings that were continually engaged and active, indicating to me "I know exactly what teacher he will do well with." Jeremy was now able to enjoy academic success as well as success on the soccer field. Even after my "fifth-year senior" had moved on from my team, I learned years later that he had done well throughout his elementary school years.

One of the joys I have had over my nearly half-century of coaching youth sports has been the notes and kind words I have received from parents. At the end of Jeremy's last season, I received a card from him and his parents. It reads as follows:

> *"Coach"-*
>
> *We cannot tell you how much we have enjoyed these past five soccer seasons, or how much we appreciate the time and effort you spend on the kids. Jeremy has really grown over the past couple of years, both on the soccer field and off, and we want to thank you for your wonderful influence on Jeremy. We will miss you and wish you the best!*

Like soccer, guiding our young people toward becoming responsible adults is a team game. Youth sports coaches many times become members of that team. Yet in Jeremy's case there were other committed members of his team. There was a school principal who took the time to get to know Jeremy and put him in the best possible setting for success. There were his parents who made the effort to hold him accountable for his behavior even at a young age. Hopefully, as he grows older, there will be others who will continue to nurture him towards a productive adult life. Chances are each of you may one day have the opportunity and privilege of getting someone you encounter off the "academically ineligible" list. All the best in that endeavor.

SAMUEL M. DENNY

MONEY DOESN'T GROW ON TREES

One of the many sayings I heard while growing up was "money doesn't grow on trees." I heard those words despite the fact that one of the local banks used the "service tree" as its company logo. I would offer that if you were to say that "money doesn't grow on trees" to a young person today, they would be in complete agreement with you. After all, they know where money comes from. If you press a button on one machine, a soft drink comes out. From a second machine, you can obtain snack food by pressing a button. And from a third machine (the ATM machine), money comes out. Or if you have a plastic card — be it a debit or credit card — you can get a lot of stuff by swiping it through. Is it any wonder that there is a disconnect by our young people and many of our adults between simply having stuff and the work (and in many cases, the increased cost) required to pay for what's been purchased?

My mother, who taught for 22 years in the local public school system, found that her calling in retirement was to provide guidance and support to the Hispanic community in our hometown of Louisville, Kentucky. Though she was not a financially sophisticated person, she was financially competent and used that knowledge to assist her Hispanic friends with money issues. One time while I was visiting with her, she noted that she thought Hispanic children had a better understanding of money than did American children. When I asked her why she thought that to be true, she answered that the Hispanic children have more opportunity to handle money and to see others handling money. For with any learned skill, mastery only comes with practice and with learning the skills in the proper order.

Financial convenience does not necessarily equate to financial competence. The ability to push a button or swipe a card does not mean that a person understands financial transactions or how to manage money. For that matter, there is no guarantee that a card user understands even basic addition and subtraction facts. As our children grow into adulthood we should offer them as many opportunities as possible to handle money in an age-appropriate manner. As adults, we can also offer our young people the opportunities to see money exchanged on a regular basis. The additional effort required may be helpful to young people and to our own financial situations as well.

SAMUEL M. DENNY

FINANCIAL MARKETS AND PSYCHOTHERAPY— A COMMON THREAD

Anyone who regularly follows the financial markets understands that account values can fluctuate up or down depending on the economic climate. It is also a given that the financial markets can be an indicator of the mood of the country at a given time. The financial indexes on Wall Street went up when Saddam Hussein was captured, went down when the president underwent a routine colonoscopy, and become nervous every time a prominent monetary official is about to make a speech on the nation's financial health. Generally speaking, investment clients are informed that stocks can go up or down and that should their investments go down in value it is best to "ride it out" and that the markets will come back in time. Therefore, clients tend to view changes in the market as typical day-to-day financial behavior.

It intrigues me that many of the trends that people accept in their financial lives are not nearly as acceptable in their personal lives. If someone we know was to demonstrate mood swings on a regular basis, we might suggest that he or she seek out help from a mental health professional. For what is termed fluctuations or cycles in the financial world could be termed as anything from depressed to manic-depressive as pertains to our personal relationships. When the mental health professional is brought in, the ultimate goal is to stabilize the behavior through counseling and/or medication. If this is the accepted and proven way to best deal with our emotional health, wouldn't it follow that the same approach should be taken as to our financial health?

During the financial crisis of 2008 I had opportunity to share notes with a long-time local news columnist. He told me at that time that there was one industry that he knew was doing a great deal better than it had prior to the crisis. When I asked him what industry that was, he replied, "the psychiatric profession." As people had seen their financial situation become "depressed," they in turn became emotionally depressed. The columnist added that the biggest spike in clients had come from one particular group. When I questioned him as to what group that was, he responded that the group was professional financial advisors. Why? The advisors had the double burden of losses in their personal accounts as well as their clients' accounts.

The healthiest way to work toward financial stability is through sustained effort toward a predictable outcome. For in a very real sense, consistency and predictability could as the old saying goes be "the apple a day that keeps the doctor away."

PROM NIGHT

Regardless of where we are in life today, many of us can recall the night of our high school prom. The prom was one of several events during senior year that signified the end of one chapter of life and the beginning of another. I was not in attendance at my high school's Senior Prom for a number of reasons; a lack of self-confidence being a primary issue. But ultimately the fact that my family was struggling financially made committing a large amount of money toward one night of my life totally impractical. I do not remember doing anything special the night of the prom. Yet what struck me the morning after the prom was that I did not feel that I had missed out by not being there.

Over the next several years, I traveled a path that many follow: I attended and graduated from college, I became established in a career, I married and started a family, and I became involved in several volunteer activities. Yet over that time period, I still found it difficult to get past some of the struggles I associated with the high school years. As my 20-year high school reunion approached, an invitation was sent for me to attend, as well as a request to see if I would help with the planning. Despite some reservations, I said yes and to my surprise, I had the opportunity of connecting with old classmates in a different way than while in school. The one thing that remained for me was to get up the courage to ask for a date — that date being my wife Linda who graciously accepted my invitation.

The evening of the reunion event was a memorable one. I was pleasantly surprised by the number of people who remembered and welcomed me. I was also surprised by the number of classmates in attendance and how well the events had been planned. Midway through the evening, I realized why the evening was special. This was the night of MY prom. This was not about the end of something, but the beginning of a number of opportunities to connect with old classmates. Maybe I had to wait 20 years for that special night in my life, but I left the reunion with a sense of completion and inner peace as to the high school years which has remained with me to this day.

Since that time, I have attended each subsequent class reunion. As before I have been remembered and welcomed. And I have also had the honor of taking Linda, my wife and date for a lifetime. Yet I still have one small struggle that perhaps classmates could give me counsel and guidance on. This past fall I asked Linda to the homecoming football game. She turned me down.

SAMUEL M. DENNY

THE COUNSEL OF KOBE BRYANT

In early 2020, sports fans and the world at large mourned the tragic death of Kobe Bryant at the age of 41. Retired from the National Basketball Association four years earlier, Kobe Bryant had carved out an active and fulfilling life. He delved into writing children's books, became an Academy-Award-winning producer, and remained active with the Los Angeles Lakers while still enjoying time with his wife and daughters. Kobe Bryant's influence was felt in a number of areas in American life. Yet it has often been overlooked that Kobe Bryant has also provided some financial wisdom we all can learn from.

I recently came across an article written about Kobe Bryant just prior to his retirement from the NBA. The article covered the entirety of Kobe's life, from his early years, the highs and lows of his life personally and professionally, and finally his decision to retire from basketball. A central theme of the story revolved around how once Kobe had become wealthy, his parents and his two sisters repeatedly came to him for money. With tears in his eyes, Kobe detailed how he had found it necessary to cut off all financial ties with his extended family. While his sisters adjusted and became fully productive adults, Kobe found himself estranged from his parents as a result of the boundary he had set. Kobe Bryant summed up his experience with the following observation:

"YOU HAVE TO GET THE MONEY OUT OF THE RELATIONSHIP!"

Kobe Bryant had to weigh a number of issues as to dealing with his extended family. First, he had to consider to what extent passing money on to his parents and his sisters would affect his personal financial future. From there he considered whether he was enabling his extended family, as opposed to being supportive. What remained was a question that has created a dilemma for numerous families—how can financial support be provided to family members and yet keep money out of the relationship?

I recall a retired couple whose daughter asked them for a loan to help her through a difficult time financially. After determining that making the loan would not jeopardize their future, the couple agreed to provide the loan with terms of repayment to be addressed at a later date. When the daughter's finances had stabilized, terms of repayment were agreed on. As opposed to payment being made to the parents, instead the money was to be given to the church that the daughter attended on a regular basis. Surprised and pleased as to the terms, within the week the daughter made arrangements to begin giving to her church. As for the retired couple, the father indicated that he had also read and learned from the Kobe Bryant article and that "it just felt like the right thing to do."

I never had opportunity to meet Kobe Bryant. But as a financial professional I hope that his counsel will help more people going forward. There may be other young persons who will be held financially accountable for a loan—but in a way that enriches both them and a worthwhile organization they care about. There may be another retired couple that will be given the needed permission to take money out of a family relationship. And there may be another worthwhile organization receiving financial support that would not have received it otherwise.

There is an old saying from my growing-up years that states "never a borrower nor lender be." Yet in life we are always borrowing or lending in everyday situations, whether within or outside of money. Those of us who recognize that fact will be those who will have the greatest personal fulfillment. And Kobe, by the way, many thanks for the loan!

SAMUEL M. DENNY

NEVER BET ON A SURE THING

When I was in the ninth grade I took as one of my courses a class in introductory Algebra. In the class I had the benefits of both highly motivated classmates and an excellent teacher. I was learning a great deal of information, but at the same time I became somewhat cocky as to my newly attained knowledge— especially around my family. My father in particular was concerned about this and began looking for a way to give me an "attitude adjustment." The way in which he brought my attitude back down to earth I have never forgotten.

Though no one in my family gambled with money, we would at times "bet" each other as to who was right about a particular idea or topic. My father, who was an accountant by profession, always thought through what he was about to bet on to be sure that he would win. So when one night at dinner he bet me that my brother (who was in the sixth grade) knew as much algebra as I did I was caught a bit off guard. But thinking that this was a bet that I had no chance of losing I readily accepted the wager. To prove that my brother could solve algebra problems, my father had me give him problems to see if he could solve for the answers. And so I began, "$2x + 3 = 7$. What is x?"

"Two," my brother answered without hesitation.

A bit taken aback, I gave my brother another problem. "$4y + 4 = 24$. What is y?"

"Five," my brother answered again without hesitating.

Still determined to prove that I was right, I gave my brother a more difficult problem. "$6y - 12 = 42$. What is y?"

My brother thought a minute, then answered with quiet confidence, "Nine."

And so it went. My brother continued to give the correct answer for each problem I gave him until I finally conceded defeat and acknowledged that my father had won the bet. It was only later in the meal that I learned the source of my brother's vast knowledge of beginning algebra. My father had given my brother the answers to the problems by giving him hand signals, the signals all the while hidden from my view by the dinner tablecloth. The number of fingers he showed my brother was equal to the correct answer to any given problem. And my brother, always open to an opportunity to show up his older sibling, was a very willing partner in the deception. From an academic standpoint, my father may have lost the bet, but rest assured he won in his efforts to relieve me of my air of superiority.

In our financial lives as well as our personal lives, things are not always as they seem. Decisions need to be made both with confidence in our abilities and humility knowing that there may be another approach that is more appropriate. And it always helps to have a resource whether personal and/or professional who can help support us with our decisions. It also does not hurt to know a bit about algebra as well.

ON FINANCIAL WINDFALLS

Chances are you have heard about or know of someone who has come into a large amount of money. Often referred to as windfalls, the monetary amount can be derived from a variety of sources. There are persons who have won the lottery by buying a ticket at a local convenience store. There are athletes and entertainers who suddenly are earning large sums of money by virtue of their talent. There are people who come into money via an inheritance. And then there are the more common ways one's financial situation can change such as a promotion at work with an accompanying large increase in salary. Most of us view a windfall as a chance to do things for ourselves and/or others that we have not had opportunity to do before. Yet sometimes in so doing we may find that our lives are not nearly as tranquil and fulfilling as before.

It has been my experience that the benefit received from a financial windfall has less to do with the amount of money received and more about the way the money is used upon receipt. Years ago prior to my daughter entering college I actually received two financial windfalls. One took the form of an inheritance received after my father's aunt passed away. The other took the form of a work opportunity that allowed me to earn a great deal of one-time additional income. The money afforded my family the opportunity to do some things we had not been able to do before, yet many of the decisions were made with an eye to the future. Both my daughter and my son could now attend college without incurring debt. We were able to remodel our kitchen and put energy-efficient windows in our home. A portion of the money was donated to our church as a one-time gift. And a portion was put away for retirement. Yet there was also thought as to the present. I gave each member of the family $300 — a total of four gifts — and told them to spend it on anything they wanted "as long as it was legal." Such were the changes in my family's financial life.

Yet a number of things did NOT change as a result of my good fortune. We continued to live in the same home. We continued to drive the same cars. We continued to interact socially with the same people that we had before. My wife and I continued to go to work as we had before. And we continued to manage our money in the same way that we had prior to our financial windfall. To quote an old saying, our goal was not to "keep up with the Jones'" but neither did we want to lose a friendship with the "Jones'" either.

Perhaps the best way to handle financial windfalls in a healthy manner is to always be aware of the smaller opportunities to improve our financial situation. Such as giving up a pack-a –day cigarette habit. Such as selling old items or collections that we no longer have use for. Such as cutting our own grass as opposed to hiring a lawn service. And such as eating together at home as a family, which will improve relationships as well as the pocketbook. For whatever one chooses to do, taking full advantage of the numerous smaller opportunities afforded us will help us retain perspective in our financial lives. And when the windfall does come, we will be able to handle it with a healthy mixture of excitement and serenity.

SAMUEL M. DENNY

ATHLETIC SHOES AND OTHER NECESSITIES OF LIFE

Before there were Nike and Reebok athletic shoes, there were Red-Ball Jets and PF Fliers available for those seeking out "tennis shoes." Both brands marketed to kids using two one-minute commercials over the space of a half hour television show. As a boy who was looking to gain an edge over the other boys in my neighborhood, I was intrigued when the ad for PF Fliers promised that I would "run faster and jump higher" if I bought their brand of shoes. When it came time for me to get a new pair of tennis shoes, I begged my parents to get me a pair of PF Fliers. My parents soon took me to get fitted for new tennis shoes and I came home excited that I now owned a brand-new pair of PF Fliers. I was now confident that I could run faster and jump higher than any other boy in the neighborhood.

The PF Fliers looked nice and were comfortable to wear. Yet almost immediately I was disillusioned when I discovered that my athletic skills had not improved as a result of the purchase. My friend who lived next door could still run faster and jump higher than I could. The stark reality simply was that he was more athletic than I was special shoes or no special shoes. I continued to wear the PF Fliers until it was time to buy the next pair of tennis shoes. I do not remember what brand of shoe was purchased, but I do know that the decision was based solely on the appearance and comfort of the shoes.

As an adult, it amazes me as to how companies market on television today. It becomes particularly confusing when watching a sporting event on network television. Over the course of five minutes I have to sort through ads from several car companies who claim to be best in "initial customer satisfaction," have to decide which light beer if any tastes best and is less filling, have to decide which after-shave is the most refreshing, and have to determine which erectile dysfunction drug I want my doctor to prescribe. And when the investment company comes on with their ad I become all the more confused, for if I purchase all the other products that have been presented to me I simply will have no money to invest. My wife in particular will not be happy with that outcome. After all, there will be no money to allow her to make decisions as to the multiple products and ads she is exposed to while watching her favorite talk shows or game shows.

How many purchases have we made whether as a child or as an adult that, while the items were of quality, did not meet the inner need we felt at the time? Perhaps the answer comes from a concept that is taught in elementary school social studies. The concept is that of BASIC human needs. All humans need food — not necessarily eating out regularly, clothing — not necessarily the latest designer brands, shelter — not necessarily a spacious house in a high-end neighborhood, and most importantly that we are loved and valued for who we are. For if one knows that they are loved and are secure in that love, it follows that somehow the other basic needs will be addressed. And from that love will follow both appreciation and discernment as to the extras we have in life.

TOO HIGH AND RIGHT DOWN THE MIDDLE

During my son 's high school years he played on a competitive club soccer team in addition to playing for his high school soccer team. One of his teammates on the club soccer team was a boy named Karlheinz Williams. While my son's skills were more suited to playing defense, Karlheinz played more up-front as a scorer. Karlheinz had a number of skills that made him well-suited to scoring goals. He was fast, had good foot skills, and was able to get himself in position to attempt to score. Yet when Karlheinz shot at the goal, he always missed with his shot too high and right down the middle. The coaches worked with Karlheinz all season long trying to teach him to kick the ball lower and into the corner of the goal. But no matter how hard Karlheinz and the coaches tried, Karlheinz continued to shoot too high and right down the middle when trying to score.

As the club soccer season drew to a close, I couldn't help but wonder if Karlheinz's tendency to shoot high and down the middle would get in the way of his progress in soccer. After that season Karlheinz and my son went their separate ways in sports. For my son, it was as a soccer player, winning all-district and all-region honors twice in high school. Yet for Karlheinz it turned out to be a different path, for when he reached high school the football team needed a place-kicker who could kick the ball high and down the middle. Karlheinz went out for the football team and as a senior was chosen on the first-team All-State squad as the top place-kicker in the state of Kentucky. The same tendencies that had hindered Karlheinz on the soccer field were an asset on the football field as he was a key contributor to a state champion football team.

More than once I have heard it said to young people that they can "be anything they want to be." Yet each of us has been given abilities in some areas but not in others. What can be most frustrating to adults and young people alike is when, like Karlheinz, you have skills that almost fit a particular situation but are not an exact fit no matter how hard one tries. It is the job of educators to help students learn where they "fit" in the adult world. For employers, it is about putting employees in the best possible position for both employee and company to thrive. And for parents, it is about knowing your child's tendencies and being open to situations where those tendencies can be best nurtured.

In our personal and in our financial lives sometimes we may find ourselves like Karlheinz. We may have good speed and good foot skills, but when it comes time to shoot at the goal we wonder why we keep missing. Perhaps instead of continually trying to maneuver into scoring position we simply need to put the ball down, take a step back, and like a good place-kicker shoot at the goal high and right down the middle. And any top-notch place-kicker benefits from having a good team around him while taking the kick.

INVESTING 101
(AS TAUGHT BY MY FATHER,
WALLER SAM DENNY)

When I was 15 years old I was given my first experience with invest-ments. Under my father's guidance I purchased 10 shares of a uranium stock at 3 ⁷/₈ per share. Within a short period of time the stock had more than doubled and reached a peak of 8 ¼ per share. Pleased with this outcome, I wanted to purchase more stock feeling that the upward trend would continue. However, my father discouraged me from doing so. He told me that my small investment could go down as rapidly as it had gone up and that it would be best to observe how the stock did over a longer period of time. Following his advice, I continued to check the financial section of the newspaper as to the progress of my investment.

Within two years my stock began to decline steadily, eventually reaching the point where the value was less than the original purchase price. Finally, my father sold the stock at a value of 2 ⁵/₈ per share. At age 17 I had my first (and only) experience losing money in the stock market. Yet just as he had done earlier, my father was there to provide guidance. I was given back the original purchase value of 3 ⁷/₈ per share with my father absorbing the loss. Immediately I put the money into my savings ac-count happy with now having a predictable outcome for my money. I had learned a valuable lesson about finances (and life in general). The lesson was simple — "don't risk what you can't afford to lose."

Unfortunately, many adults have made investment decisions similar to mine on a much larger scale that have caused stress in both their financial and personal lives. At that point, there is no longer the caring parent to guide and to perhaps absorb the blow. And many of us have taken similar risks in areas of life outside of money — our health, our relationships, our personal integrity — that we have come to regret later. My father had me take a small financial risk as a young person to help me understand what could be lost as well as gained from making investments. Yet at the same time my father invested in me by modeling for me the importance of being honorable both morally and financially.

There is no stock market index that can measure the loss when one abuses their body. There is no stock market index that can measure the loss when one does not work toward healthy relationships with others. Yet there is a measurement as to the loss of personal integrity that unlike stock indexes is simple and straightforward. As a business colleague of mine once said to me:

"Integrity is like virginity. You can only lose it once."

ABOUT FOOTBALL COACHES, BUBBLE GUM CARDS, AND REUNIONS

During my years at Seneca High School the football coach was Ron Cain, who led Seneca to the state football championship in 1965 and a runner-up finish in 1968. During the championship season Coach Cain was my teacher for ninth-grade health class. One day during class (which that day consisted of polishing our skills on the basketball court) Coach Cain told me that prior to going into teaching he had tried out for and made the Denver Broncos team during the initial season of the old American Football League. He also told me that he had never actually played due to injury sustained prior to the start of the season. Though I always remembered him sharing that part of his life with me, I did not give it a great deal of thought until years later.

Around 1989 I was shopping at a sports card shop as I did on a periodic basis. While there I noticed four 1960 Fleer football cards of a player named Ronnie Cain. Curious, I read the back of the cards and concluded that it was indeed Coach Cain from Seneca. I purchased all four of the cards at fifty cents apiece and over time bought additional cards of the coach as I was able to locate them. Shortly afterward my wife Linda had her 20-year high school reunion. I took one of the cards to the reunion and showed it to a number of people there. Virtually everyone (including those who had played for him) was unaware of his being on a professional football roster. I took the card to my 30-year high school reunion in 1999 and again people were surprised to learn of his time in professional football. Regardless, it intrigued me as to why he had thought to tell me what he apparently had told very few people.

In 2000, Linda and I attended her 30-year high school reunion. Again, I took the card of Coach Cain with me. As before, I began showing the card to a number of people there. Then about halfway through the function Linda flagged me down and told me someone wanted to see me about my football card. I was taken to meet a woman standing outside the auditorium. The woman then introduced herself to me, "I'm Phyllis Cain. I would love to see your card. Our family used to have one, but one of our grandchildren lost it a few years ago." The card had been a family treasure, having become more so after Coach Cain had passed away. I handed her the card and told her she could keep it if she wanted. Initially she declined, but then upon my insistence accepted it. Three weeks later I received the following letter from Phyllis:

Dear Sam,

Words cannot express how much recovering Ron's football card meant to me and our children/grandchildren. The four-year-old clasped the card to his chest and said "I'm keeping this, it's my Big Daddy." I had to wait until he was distracted to retrieve the card. We don't want to lose this one.

Ron and I had wonderful memories of our years at Seneca High—it was the best of times. We still cry at times over losing big Ron. Phil Thompson said it best, "Ron was hard to love but we loved him dearly."

Thank you so very much, we are forever grateful for your kindness.

Sincerely,

Phyllis Cain

Since that time, as I have been able to locate additional cards of Coach Cain, I have been in contact with Phyllis as to who she would want to have a card. I was able to get cards to all three of their children, all four of their grandchildren, their nephew who played in the NFL, and a number of former players (several of whom played on the state champion team). A signature moment for Phyllis came when in the fall of 2010 Seneca invited back the members of the 1965 state champion football team. And in 2013 Phyllis and her family were present when the football stadium was named in honor of Coach Cain. During both events, she was able to reconnect with a number of people from that time in her life. Though I never played a down of football while at Seneca, I find it interesting that a brief conversation with one of my teachers years ago could have taken me down such an interesting and fulfilling journey.

As appeared in *Sports Collectors Daily* (6-12-2016)

SAMUEL M. DENNY

FOOD FOR THOUGHT
(OR "TELL A LIE IN LOVE")

When my grandmother was 85 years old she had to enter a nursing home as a result of a broken hip, spending the remaining seven years of her life there. During the first year that she was there, the family noticed that she had become depressed as the Christmas season was drawing near. My grandmother had always enjoyed buying gifts for her family during the holiday season, but now her income had to be used to pay for the cost of her care. For some time, I wondered what could be done to boost her spirits. The answer came to me when I remembered a story she had told me years before.

While Grandmother was still in her home students from a local school came by selling raffle tickets with the prize being a large basket of groceries. Grandmother purchased two tickets—one in her name and one in the name of a neighbor. When the drawing took place, the ticket with the neighbor's name on it was drawn out. Yet when the grocery basket was distributed, the neighbor neither gave Grandmother a share of the groceries nor paid her for the ticket. Grandmother had never forgotten the slight. And when just before Christmas two girls from a neighborhood Catholic school came by our home to sell raffle tickets—this time with three cash prizes being awarded—an idea came to me.

Third prize for this particular raffle was $100. So, I went to the neighborhood Catholic school with a $100 bill and asked the school to make out a check to my grandmother in that amount. After getting the check, I went to visit my grandmother at the nursing home as I did on a weekly basis. I told her that I had bought two raffle tickets for a chance on a cash prize—one in my name and one in her name. I also told her that the drawing had taken place and her ticket had been drawn out for the $100.00 third prize. At that point, I handed the check to her. Again I heard the story about the raffle for the basket of groceries, but this time I detected a difference in the way she told it. In her eyes matters had finally been righted for the slight she had received years before. And getting the check did indeed relieve the depression she had felt up until that time.

I had told my grandmother a lie. Not a half-truth. Not even a quarter truth. But an outright lie. Yet when I left her that day I couldn't help but feel good about the story I had told her. Perhaps that is because often the most meaningful gifts are those where the giver's identity is disguised or unknown. How many times have people simply bought gifts and not thought about the most meaningful way to make the gift? For as with my grandmother, the way in which the gift is given may actually have more benefit that the gift itself.

ABOUT SETTING GOALS

Not long ago, my high school in Louisville, KY sent a message to alumni asking for volunteers to assist students with "goal setting" for their future. As I have done volunteer work with public school students, I am fully aware of educators wanting to make their students "college and career ready." Yet I am also aware that often our young people have goals that are not fully compatible with what the adults in their lives envision for them.

In giving thought as to what I would say to a young person as to "goal setting" I would first share some of my own struggles when I was at their point in life. From there I would offer what I hope would be a foundation of primary goals to be built upon in the future.

SHOWING UP: In other words, make sure to always be present both physically and mentally. Years ago, while mentoring a high school student who played on the baseball team, I shared with him the story of Cal Ripken playing in a record 2632 consecutive games. Cal Ripken did not miss a day of work for over 16 years – his teammates knew that he would be both physically present and mentally engaged each day. All of us have a responsibility to "show up" whether that be our families, our places of employment, or our outside commitments. And "showing up" leads to another relevant goal:

NIELS—"WITH RESPECT." Most of us remember when we received our high school yearbook and asked our friends to sign. What my classmate Niels Fogt wrote by his picture remains with me to this day. The message was simply "Niels—with respect." This came from a person who fully understood the difference between being popular and being respected. Niels earned respect by giving complete effort whether as a student or as a key member of a talented football team. What followed was that Niels also was well-liked by all who knew him. Among other things, respect entails accepting and embracing our differences as well as the ways in which we are alike. The person who does so will be able to function well in a variety of life situations.

LUCK . . . LOVE . . . LAUGHTER. Another of the messages written to me in my high school yearbook was written by a schoolmate who I also attended church with. After writing the usual well-wishes, she ended with the words "luck . . . love . . . laughter." The depth of thought struck me at the time and even more so later on when I learned that life during high school had not been kind to her and her family. Her message brings to our attention three tools that when used wisely will enrich the lives of all those we encounter:

> LUCK is being aware that all of us are presented with opportunities What makes those opportunities "luck" is taking full advantage and utilizing them for the benefit of all.

> LOVE begins with accepting yourself fully. Doing so will allow you to accept and receive love, whether that love is romantic, or given to you in the form of accountability, or being supported when you are unable to go it on your own.

> LAUGHTER enriches our lives and our physical health as well. When you laugh, always remember to be laughing with others and not at the expense of others.

It goes without saying that all of our young people will do better in life if they have a clear set of goals, now and for the future. May we as adults always be willing to provide the guidance and foundation that will allow them to reach their goals.

SAMUEL M. DENNY

YOUR CHILD'S CAREER CHANGE

Most people who have spent significant time in the American work force have at some point dealt with the possibility of losing their job, which is what the corporate world refers to as "downsizing." For many it has meant a change of lifestyle as well as a change in career. Being a good employee and dedicating one's life to the company does not protect a person from the proverbial pink slip. Even those who do remain in their jobs face often higher demands and increased workloads from their supervisors, causing them to wonder if indeed there is something better out there for them. Yet it is human nature to remain with what is familiar even when it is not beneficial to do so.

It strikes me as interesting that while many adults face sudden changes in career and lifestyle, all of our young people at some point will be facing a layoff notice from society. Since the age of five, their job title has been "student." Just as with adults in the working world, they are called in periodically for a performance review that is referred to as a "report card." The pay is referred to as "grades" as opposed to a salary. Ironically, the more experience one gains in a career as a student, the sooner one will get a layoff notice from the educational system, either after high school or college graduation. Regardless of when the layoff notice is given, it is as if one has been fired after being a good employee since the age of five. And there is no age discrimination law on the books that addresses the sudden career change from student to adult.

For many young people a good education is a must in order to integrate into the work force. Yet it is even more important to emphasize to our young people the fulfillment that comes with being able to fully support yourself financially through honorable work. Upon graduation from college I did not immediately enter a career, but worked to support myself doing a variety of jobs. I delivered three large newspaper routes, cut grass, delivered circulars, and tutored elementary school children. In combination, I was able to pay my living expenses and save some money. Knowing what it took both time-wise and financially to support myself proved beneficial in ultimately choosing a career. And many of the skills required in my financial services career are skills developed when my career was simply learning how to become a self-supporting young adult.

While the value of a quality education should be emphasized to our young people, it is more important to teach our young people to appreciate all kinds of honorable work and to not look at certain jobs as "beneath them." Just as we need doctors, lawyers, and corporate executives we also need mechanics, custodial workers, and sanitation workers in American society. As it was put to me by a friend of mine with a 10th grade formal education and a PhD in living a productive life, "there are people with college degrees that don't even know how to change their own oil." And making sure the oil is changed in your car — whether by you or someone you trust — is just one of many tasks required to function in today's adult world.

PATHWAY TO SUCCESS

A tradition for each senior class in my high school was to choose a boy and a girl class member for a number of "superlatives." Included among the list of superlatives were "most intelligent," "most athletic," "most creative," and especially "most likely to succeed." Chosen as the girl from my graduating class as "most likely to succeed" was Sherry (Johns) Spence. During her high school years, Sherry consistently demonstrated the enthusiasm and work ethic that are essential to success in life. Yet perhaps her strongest asset was her ability to recognize a problem and from there use the resources available to her to come up with a positive result, even back when as a sixth grader, Sherry, participated in the Bashford Manor Elementary School talent show.

Sherry's act for the school talent show was a rendition of "Moon River," a 1963 hit song written by legendary composer Henry Mancini and made a hit by singer Andy Williams. As was her personality, Sherry walked onto the stage fully prepared for her moment in the spotlight. But as Sherry burst into song it became apparent that this was a performance that people would remember, as opposed to a memorable performance. Put more simply, Sherry had not been gifted with even a speck of natural musical talent.

Yet it was at this moment that Sherry put to use the skills that would make her successful in life. To start, she too recognized — midway through the song — that her future was not going to be as a professional vocalist. Thereafter, she determined that to have a stable long-term future she would need to get more serious about school. Finally, she made a commitment to herself to fully utilize the resources available to her in order to achieve a successful outcome.

Sherry was an outstanding student during her high school years, yet classwork was not all of her involvement in school life. She was active on the yearbook staff, served on the student council, was president of the

Future Teachers of America, and was a member of several class executive boards. After high school, Sherry completed her college education and evolved into a successful long-term career in personnel management for two large corporations, retiring at the age of 49. At present, Sherry enjoys family and friends as well as the benefits of a comfortable retirement.

Success in life is something all of us aspire to. Yet often the beginning of the pathway to success is initial failure. What we learn from failure also determines our future. Perhaps in a way life is a long-term series of courses as to managing failure. Graduation, whether at school or in life, ultimately comes but one way — by achieving full awareness of our limitations as well as our strengths.

THE CROWD MENTALITY

Recently I had the opportunity to reconnect with Ron Wolford, a boyhood friend who I had not seen for almost fifty years. Our families lived next door to each other and we had interacted in a number of ways. At present Ron is a homebuilder. On his website it states that he began his career upon graduation from college. Yet as we recalled old times, I reminded Ron that his career really began in the summer of 1961 when we both were ten years of age.

That summer Ron Wolford organized a group of neighborhood boys to build a baseball diamond (and a figure-eight track) in the field behind both our houses. The baseball diamond had inset bases, base lines cut out from dirt that extended into the outfield, grass that was mowed regularly by Ron, and finally a wooden backstop that eliminated the need for a catcher. Most days that summer, boys of all ages gathered to play pickup baseball on the newly built field. And each of us felt a particular degree of pride as to the sturdily constructed backstop that stood behind home plate.

One day late that summer, we discovered that the prized wooden backstop had been knocked over, making it more difficult to keep a baseball in the playing area than before. All of us who had come to play were upset and wondered who had toppled the backstop, as well as how and why. At that moment, Ron as our leader spoke up and indicated that he thought a boy named Joey was the guilty party. Since Joey did not play baseball with the rest of us, it stood to reason that perhaps his feelings had been hurt by not being included.

The collective frustration of a group of neighborhood boys was now directed at Joey. We had all worked hard to build the backstop and did not appreciate our efforts going for naught. Yet it was at this point that I began using ten-year-old logic and wondered if Joey could have actually done it. To begin with, Joey was only three years old, was constantly being watched by his grandmother, and never allowed to leave his yard. Even if Joey had been able to leave his yard, he was not nearly big enough to have toppled the backstop by himself. Finally, I realized that even though I was much bigger than Joey, I was unable to move the backstop solely by my own efforts.

There was now genuine doubt in my mind as to Joey's guilt. Yet I didn't have the moral courage at that age to speak out in Joey's defense. After all, Ron Wolford was a leader in the neighborhood who as a rule stuck up for the underdog. So I deferred to Ron and to the group at large. If Ron said Joey did it—HE DID IT!

Fortunately, no action was taken by the group and we simply reset the backstop and continued playing baseball. As it turned out, the collective feeling towards Joey was largely due to his grandmother being protective of him to the point of not always acting in a pleasant manner toward the neighborhood boys. Becoming older allowed all of us to better understand why Joey's grandmother had been so protective. And to our surprise, his grandmother became more amiable towards us as Joey got older.

How many times in life have we found strong leaders making assertions that upon using logic we find their statements to be inaccurate and/or unfeeling? And unlike Ron Wolford, who soon went back to his usual demeanor of sticking up for the underdog, these persons can potentially inflict long-term damage on both individuals and society at large. In a time of "change and challenge" as described by our national media, let us be open to change and be respectful of all persons and viewpoints. Doing so may well require a degree of moral courage and conviction, but the end result will be that more of us will thrive and flourish regardless of our differences.

SAMUEL M. DENNY

A GENTLEMAN ON
AND OFF THE FIELD

During my time at high school, the yearbook often had the graduating seniors select a favorite quotation to appear beside their photo. Beside my picture was the quote "great leaders are men that know their fates before other men do." While I question how well that quote described me I can certainly say that my classmate Bill Earls had a quote beside his picture that truly fit. It read:

"The flowering of civilization is the finished man, the man of sense, of grace, of accomplishment, of social power—the gentleman."

I have known Bill Earls since the first grade and we have interacted in a variety of ways over the years. Having been given a strong moral and spiritual upbringing, Bill has always been the gentleman as described in the quote. At no time did I see his social grace more in evidence than in a Senior Division Little League baseball game that we both were playing in. My team (the Reds) was at bat and Bill was playing shortstop for his team (the Mets). I had just gotten on base via a walk and was happy to be on first base given that my hitting ability was almost nonexistent. However, I did have good speed and as such was given the sign by my coach to steal second base. As the pitcher delivered his pitch, I took off for second base and stole it successfully. While sliding in I saw that the catcher had thrown the ball into centerfield and so I got up and ran to third base. In an exuberant frame of mind now that I was at third base (again, a destination I seldom reached due to my lack of hitting ability), I thought I might be able to score. It was at that point that I had a rude awakening.

As I made the big turn between third base and home plate, Bill quietly walked behind me and tagged me out. He had had the ball in his possession for some time and by using the "hidden ball trick" was just waiting for me to lose focus as to what was going on in the game. Needless to say, I was humiliated. I went to the bench not sure how my coaches and teammates would react to me. It was then that Bill set the tone so as not to embarrass me. Upon tagging me out he simply turned, threw the ball back to the pitcher, and ran back to his shortstop position. He did not taunt me or embarrass me in any way. And because of the example he set, my coaches and teammates accepted my mistake and were ready to help support me in moving forward.

In an era when taunting and trash talking seem to be on the rise in all sports, all athletes regardless of age should follow the example that was modeled by Bill Earls that day. In many ways, athletics are a teacher as to how to lead a productive life. Regardless of what the sports world often wants us to believe "life is not a zero-sum game.' May each of you be a winner in the game of life.

SAMUEL M. DENNY

BASEBALL CARDS AND THE BUSINESS OF INVESTING

Like many young boys growing up, I collected baseball cards. I started somewhat randomly, simply buying packs of cards and storing them in an empty cigar box. As I got older, I began collecting in a more organized fashion. My cards were now kept in two-drawer file cabinets my father had obtained for me and were organized by year, then in numerical order. Over time, I was able to acquire the collections of every other boy in the neighborhood; by doing so, I got a small taste of the business of mergers and acquisitions. I had stopped actively collecting baseball cards by the end of junior high school, but still owned over 11,000 cards from the mid 1950's to the mid 1960's. Needless to say, my mother did NOT throw my cards away.

As a young adult and needing some immediate cash, I sold my collection for over three times the money I had put into it. Several years later, my wife bought me some packs of baseball cards as a gift and that got me back into collecting. Over the next ten years, I rebuilt my card collection to over 40,000 cards. Also during that time, baseball card collecting began to evolve from a kid's hobby into a miniature stock market. I met more than one grown man who, armed with a baseball card price guide, was purchasing cards with the intent of funding his child's college education or paying off his mortgage.

My intent, on the other hand, was simply the enjoyment of reconnecting with my childhood. But after some time, a small voice in my head began telling me that again I needed to sell my collection. So I sold my baseball card collection a second time at a price that enabled me to purchase a new car and have new carpet put in our home.

Shortly after that the baseball card market began to tank. Cards printed in the 1980's and 1990's reached the status of "junk bonds" due to overproduction. Adults who had counted on baseball cards as an investment for the future saw their "portfolios" shrink in a manner comparable to the stock market decline during the Great Depression. Though I was knowledgeable about the value of baseball cards, to this day I don't know how I intuitively knew to sell my collection at that time. Regardless, my family benefited greatly from my "investment activity" during that time and my sense of when to sell.

It seems to me that when adults invest in the real world, sometimes we expect too much from our financial advisors. There are many competent professionals who can explain how investment products work, but fewer who have an intuitive feel for how an investment product is going to perform. While on two occasions I was able to profit on an investment, my baseball card collection was intended to be an enjoyable hobby as opposed to the cornerstone of my family's financial future. I have again rebuilt my collection, this time to well over 100,000 cards. Whether this collection will be sold at a later date remains to be seen. Regardless, perhaps the wisest counsel as to managing one's resources—whether it be baseball cards or financial portfolios—comes from the New Testament of the Christian Bible:

"—for where your treasures are, there will your heart be also."

SAMUEL M. DENNY

ABOUT KIDS, POLITICS, AND BASEBALL

Awhile back, I had the pleasure and privilege of reconnecting with Barbara Barnstable Edelman at our high school Hall of Fame dinner. Barbara was one of the inductees based on an outstanding career as an attorney and civic leader. What I most respect about Barbara is the balance she seems to maintain between family and career. A few months afterwards, Barbara and I had opportunity to exchange stories about our families that revolved around small children and political views. The story I shared with Barbara is as follows:

"As for my granddaughter Rose, there is a story that with all respect to your political views would like to pass on. On June 14 of last year my daughter went to the hospital to have labor induced that morning with the expectation that a very large baby would be born that evening. However, Rose waited until 3:30 on the morning of June 15 to enter the world at a not-so-small 9 pounds 11 ounces. That day my granddaughter Rose became perhaps the youngest person ever to make a strong political statement. By deciding to enter the world at the time she did she made it clear that she did not want to share a birthday with our current president. Instead she chose to honor her mother by sharing her birthday with Dusty Baker, the first baseball player that her mother recognized when but two years of age. Hopefully Rose will continue to have a strong sense of our country's political climate. Only time will tell."

Barbara, in turn, shared the following story about her family with me:

"While not completely on topic your story reminds me of a good story though. Years ago when my kids who are now 33, 31, and 31 were five, three, and three there was a program in Lexington to encourage parents to teach their kids to vote.

It was called Kids Vote. You took your kids to the polls with you on election day and they had a small voting booth for little kids and they got to vote.

All three of mine voted. After we got back in the car I asked Kevin the oldest who he had voted for. He told me George Bush. I asked our daughter Laura who she voted for and she told me Bill Clinton. I asked our youngest son Mitchell who he voted for and he said Pete Rose. I was quite shocked but thought maybe that wasn't such a bad idea after all. Then after I thought about it I realized he had voted for Ross Perot. We still think Pete Rose would have made a good one."

Knowing Barbara, I suspect she took full advantage of another teachable moment after she got her children in the car. I can picture her using her skills as an attorney to get each of her children to say why they had voted for the candidate they had chosen. I can also hear the mother in Barbara offering her children a lesson as to respecting viewpoints that might differ from their own. As for Dusty Baker and Pete Rose, I suspect both of them would be honored to know that some of our voting population felt that baseball skills were readily transferable into the political realm. Regardless, perhaps what both my granddaughter Rose and the Edelman family have modeled for all of us is that big changes begin with small steps. May we all be willing to take those steps now and in the future.

SAMUEL M. DENNY

THE FABLE OF THE TORTOISE AND THE HARE—FOR TODAY

Anyone who has read Aesop's Fables probably remembers the story of "The Tortoise and the Hare" in which an overconfident hare challenges a tortoise to a race. The hare jumps out to a big lead over the tortoise, but then feeling he has the race won, he stops to take a nap. When the hare awakens, he finds to his dismay that the tortoise passed him while he was asleep and has already crossed the finish line. The moral to this particular fable is simply "slow and steady wins the race."

Given the times in which we live, if the story were to be told today it might go like this:

One day a hare, supremely confident in his ability to run fast, challenged a tortoise to a race. The tortoise agreed on the condition that the race would be an all-day race as opposed to a sprint. The hare's strategy was to run erect using the wind to help push him forward. The tortoise, on the other hand, chose to move forward staying as low to the ground as possible. When the race began, the hare sprinted out to a big lead, aided by a strong wind at his back. But after a while, the wind shifted directions and began to push the hare backwards. The wind continued to push the hare backwards for the next several hours. When the wind finally began to die down, the hare noticed that the tortoise had progressed over twice as far as he had.

After a time, the wind again began to blow forward, enabling the hare to narrow the tortoise's lead to but a few yards. But yet again the wind reversed course and pushed the hare backwards at far greater force than before. Upon the wind subsiding the hare noticed to his dismay that he had now been pushed to a point behind the original starting line of the race. The tortoise, on the other hand, continued to progress slowly and consistently forward by keeping his body as low to the ground as possible. The hare after a time was again able to move forward, but this time the wind

83

he had counted on to push him ahead was but a slight breeze.

As the race neared its end, the hare had narrowed the gap between himself and the tortoise by a small margin. However, the tortoise still held a commanding lead having covered almost twice as much ground as the hare. The hare still retained hopes of catching the tortoise, but he was also fearful that yet a third strong wind would push him back causing him to lose part or all of the ground he had covered. The tortoise continued to move steadily forward, never deviating from his long-term strategy for the race.

The hare's predicament in the story is where a number of people have found their financial portfolios over the years. Counting on a strong wind to aid them, they have learned that the wind can suddenly and unexpectedly change course causing them to lose part or all of the ground they had gained in the beginning. Putting money back for the future ultimately is an endurance race as opposed to a sprint. And the best strategy for running an endurance race is maintaining a consistent pace so that one will have the necessary stamina to cross the finish line a financial winner.

SAMUEL M. DENNY

WRESTLING WITH HUMILITY

When I entered high school in 1963, one of the classes I took during the first semester was a seventh-grade physical education course taught by Coach Ron Cain. The class introduced us to flag football, basketball, track, and wrestling as well as daily calisthenics. As the semester progressed, we learned who in the class was proficient in certain sports. In my case I found that I excelled in track as a middle-distance runner. As for my classmate Doug Hatfield it became apparent that he was far and away the best pound-for-pound wrestler in the class. The fact that Doug also was not lacking in self-confidence made him all the more dominating in the sport. Quick and deceptively strong, he won match after match against boys his own size.

But after a while, Doug's natural self-confidence began to evolve into a degree of cockiness. This posed a dilemma for Coach Cain as to how to give Doug an appropriate "attitude adjustment." And it was at this point that Coach Ron Cain, usually known for taking the direct approach on issues, decided to use a subtle method in dealing with Doug. So from that point forward Doug found himself wrestling against boys who were progressively bigger than he was. The hope was that the loss of a wrestling match would bring Doug's self-confidence to a more realistic level. However, Doug continued to win match after match regardless of the size of his opponent. I among others absorbed a loss to Doug on the wrestling mats. And after Doug defeated a boy named Berry Bouchee (who though not athletic was far taller and more broadly built than Doug), both Coach Cain and the class began to wonder if there was anyone who could topple Doug from his perch.

Finally, Doug was matched up against Greg Frey, who like Berry Bouchee was far taller and more broadly built than Doug. Greg was gentle in nature but did possess a degree of competitiveness and athletic ability. As the match began Doug again attempted to use his quickness and strength to gain an advantage. But this time the outcome of the match was far different. Greg Frey soon had Doug pinned to the mats and from there simply sat on him. There was absolutely no escape route for Doug and the end of the match found Greg Frey a decisive winner. Doug Hatfield absorbed two losses that day. The first was the loss of a wrestling match. The second loss was the loss of an excess amount of self-confidence which in turn allowed him to have a more realistic sense of his abilities.

During our 30- year class reunion in 1999 I had opportunity to re-connect with Doug Hatfield for a brief period of time. When I mentioned to Doug both his ability as a wrestler and his eventual loss to a much larg-er opponent he responded simply "I REMEMBER THAT!" in a way that indicated a life's lesson well learned. And as with Doug may we all have a realistic appreciation of both our abilities and the abilities of others. After all, both Coach Cain and Doug would insist.

SAMUEL M. DENNY

ON BUYING YOUR FREEDOM

Shortly after my father died my mother received the proceeds from a modest life insurance policy. About the same time, she was contacted by a stockbroker who worked for a firm that my father had done a small amount of business with. My mother set up a meeting with the stockbroker, asking my brother and me to also be present. At the meeting the stockbroker recommended a program that promised high returns but would be low-risk as to whether the account would lose money. Given that during his lifetime my father had always put money in programs that had a guaranteed outcome, I was not completely comfortable with the proposal. Yet because my mother seemed to have already made her decision, I voiced no reservations and supported her choice.

After a time, my mother called me and asked me to review the contract the stockbroker had set up. She had put additional money into the program and it had done well for a while, but now the account had lost a small amount of money as the markets had gone down. I reminded her of the risk involved but also reassured her that most of her money was in other programs that were providing her with guarantees. The stockbroker was contacted and asked to transfer her funds into a "fixed" account that would guarantee that she would not lose money. But after a few months, my mother called me again far more concerned about her account than before. For despite the assurance from the stockbroker that the account would no longer lose money, the statement still indicated a loss of funds from the prior reporting period.

My mother now wanted to get out of the program, but was afraid to due to the fact that by so doing, she would lose about $500 on her account. She then asked me both as her son and as a financial professional what to do. I struggled as to how to present the potential $500 loss in a way that would put my mothers' mind at ease. After a great deal of thought, this is what I said to her:

"Mom, I have found a program for you that will guarantee both the money you put in and interest as well. It will cost about $500 to move the money, but what you will be doing is buying your freedom. The freedom of knowing that your money is always growing. The freedom to focus fully on the things you enjoy in life. And the freedom of knowing that what you are doing with your money is consistent with your comfort level. Dad always wanted to be sure that money would be there for all of us, so he never put money where he didn't know what the outcome would be. We just need to do things the way Dad would have done it."

Following the example my father had modeled throughout his life was enough. My mother moved the money, taking the $500 loss. As a financial advisor, I saw a woman again comfortable with the way her financial resources were being managed. But as her son, I witnessed something even more important. My mother could again give freely financially and emotionally to the many people she cared about. Yet again I was reminded of the need to make sure that my clients were in a healthy relationship with their money. And more times than we realize striving for a larger portfolio does not necessarily coincide with having a healthy relationship with your financial resources.

SAMUEL M. DENNY

LEARNING DISABLED

A number of years ago a middle-aged career educator divorced her husband of 26 years. From there she relocated to a large metropolitan city
in a different state from where she had been living, changing jobs to take
a position first as an educational consultant and later as an elementary
school principal. As she continued to shape her new life she decided to
chase a lifelong dream of achieving a doctoral degree in education. Using borrowed money to fund her schooling, she pursued her degree at a
well- respected New England university. The curriculum was both highly challenging and quite expensive, but after a time she completed her
studies and was awarded her doctoral degree. It seemed that this career
educator had achieved ultimate fulfillment professionally. In her mind
the possibilities for the future seemed endless.

Fast forward to the present. This career educator is now approaching
retirement age and has been let go from her position as a school principal.
Unable to find work comparable to what she has done throughout her career, she lives with her mother in the medium-sized town where she grew
up. She earns income as a substitute teacher in the town school system, the
income being a far cry from what she had earned prior. She can only wonder how things could have changed so rapidly and so dramatically for her.

The term "learning disabled" is often used in the educational field to
describe a number of perceptual limitations found in children and adoles-
cents. But in this case "learning disabled" could well apply to this highly
educated professional woman. Initially, she failed to recognize that her
advanced education could actually limit her career options as opposed to
increasing them. With significantly less income and a high debt load, she
was no longer able to live independently. She had mortgaged her future
and by doing so had failed to accurately assess the financial implications
for her down the road.

Yet there was a second, less apparent learning disability that came into play. Despite her age and her advanced education, this career educator had never learned how to fully discern the physical and emotional boundaries of others. This was a limitation that undermined her marriage and contributed to its eventual end. It also affected her career in that despite working in the same field throughout her life, she never held any position for more than a few years. Nowhere in the course of her educational study (whether formal or otherwise) had her impairment been identified and addressed. For had her limitations been dealt with while she was a young person, life might have turned out far differently for her.

Formal education is a necessity in today's society. Yet all too often we fail to recognize that ultimately it is even more important to develop healthy interpersonal skills. No college or university offers a degree in recognizing the physical and emotional boundaries of others. It is up to us as parents, public school educators, and other involved adults to teach our young people the relationship skills they will need going forward. And those relationship skills are best taught by the example that each of us model for young and old alike.

SAMUEL M. DENNY

ON STARTING UP
A LAWN SERVICE

Before the growth of commercial lawn services, boys who lived in my neighborhood were often hired by homeowners to cut grass and/or do additional yardwork. Starting at the age of 11 I began cutting grass using a lawn mower and gasoline provided by my parents. During a typical summer, I had two yards that I was paid weekly to cut as well as the responsibility of cutting the grass at home. After several summers the family lawn mower began to break down and my father began looking for a replacement mower. Given that now I thought I had extensive experience cutting grass, I believed that I should be paid to cut the grass at home and approached my father as to what would be a fair price.

My father was open to the idea of paying me. Yet he also felt that there was a choice I needed to make. I could be paid for cutting the grass at home, but in turn I had to purchase the necessary lawn mower out of my own resources. I would also have to pay for the cost of the gasoline used, the oil that was periodically needed, and pay for any repairs on the mower. Upon being presented with the options, I withdrew money out of my savings account and purchased a brand-new Sears Craftsman lawn mower.

I was now the sole proprietor of a neighborhood lawn service. I was cutting the family yard and two other lawns once a week and being paid a competitive wage of $2.00 for each yard. I was paying for the gasoline and oil as needed and was now responsible for seeing that the mower was properly serviced. Becoming a "small business owner" in turn made me more aware of keeping the mower properly maintained and more aware of practicing good safety habits while operating the mower. Within the year I had recouped my investment costs and operated my business at a profit for a couple of years after that. Upon entering college, I passed my business on to my brother who bought the lawn mower from me and took over the lawns I had been cutting.

My father could have simply made a decision to pay me or not pay me, but instead gave me an age-appropriate opportunity to take owner-ship of a family financial decision. In an era where most decisions (finan-cial or otherwise) seem to be made on the run, perhaps we as adults need to stop and look for ways to give our young people a degree of ownership for decisions made both individually or within the family. Giving young people opportunities to take ownership of decisions in life will require thought as well as effort on the part of adults. Doing so will hopefully result in young people who have the confidence to make their own way in life both financially and emotionally.

SAMUEL M. DENNY

FIRST MAN OFF THE BENCH

During my senior year at Seneca High School I participated in an intra-mural basketball league organized by the school and played at the school gym. Each team consisted of seven players and games were played week-ly. When I received my team assignment prior to the start of play I dis-covered that I was one of but two Caucasian players on the roster. The re-maining five players were of African-American descent For the first time in my life I was in a setting where I would be in the minority, despite the fact that at that time the Seneca High School student enrollment was pre-dominantly Caucasian. And right before league play started I learned that I would be even more in the minority when the other Caucasian player quit the squad. Given that I did not know any of the other five players well I was not certain what to expect. Regardless, I decided to play out the season and to fit into whatever role the team required of me.

I soon learned what my function would be on the team. I was the "first (and only) man off the bench." As the first game began I remem-ber thinking that I was going to have very little playing time. Yet as the game progressed I found I was being called on to relieve other players as they became tired and needed a break. The game ended with my having received a significant amount of playing time. As league play continued I found myself an integral part of the team coming off the bench as needed to relieve other players. The season concluded on a high note with our team of six winning the intramural league championship. And to this day I have the individual trophy from that season which I keep not so much in recognition of the athletic achievement, but more to remind me of how five African-Americans accorded fairness and respect to a minority of one as we all worked toward a common goal.

Years later, I had opportunity to reconnect with Larry Bailey, one of my teammates from that time. We both recalled playing on the team and the life lessons in cooperation we had learned and put to use. And as each of us becomes more aware of diversity both within and outside of our communities, I would like to pass on a couple of things I have observed recently. One day while visiting at Seneca High School I noticed two students having a conversation at the bus loading dock. The language being spoken was not English. At around the same time I went to my nearby branch bank to make a deposit. While waiting I witnessed an African-American teller waiting on a Caucasian woman while the other teller (who was East Indian in descent) was waiting on an Asian man. For the name of the game now is diversity as pertains to our day-to-day life. It is hoped that each of you will embrace the diversity around you and become richer because of it.

SAMUEL M. DENNY

THE IMPORTANCE OF GOOD DEFENSE

For most of my life I have served as a youth sports coach. Initially I coached Little League baseball, but later have coached youth soccer for ages 4 and 5 at the local YMCA over a period of 25 years. I never played the game of soccer and what I did know about the game came largely from watching my son play from the age of five up through high school. Yet as I got further into coaching preschool children, I found that sometimes extensive knowledge of the sport could get in the way when it came to working with beginning players. My job as coach was to build the foundation from which they could grow in the sport. And one game I was involved in a few years ago brought home to me the importance of teaching players the fundamentals of good defense.

The team we were playing that day had children of approximately the same skill level as my team did. The opposing coach was a caring and knowledgeable man who had played soccer at the college level. Each team had six players on the field. Three players were on offense with their job being to score goals. The other three players--a goalie and two "goalie helpers" — were to remain back on defense and were stationed at the goalie box. The helpers were to use the box as "base" and rotate around the edge of the box, remembering to stay between the opposing player and the goal at all times. When the game was set to begin, the opposing team was positioned similar to the way you would position a college team. The way my team was lined up was indicative of my rudimentary knowledge of the game of soccer.

Yet when the game actually began, everything changed. The opposing team's two goalie helpers did not remain on defense and were playing as if they were trying to score. This allowed my players a greater opportunity to score given there was only the goalie to stop them. On the other hand, my defenders remembered that they were to remain on base and were ready to help our goalie if needed. When the game ended my team won by the score of 8-0. The final score was in no way reflective of the ability level of the two teams. What it did indicate was the value of sound defense, for even if our team had not scored eight goals one goal would still have been enough to win.

Just as in youth sports and sports at every level it is important to play good position defense in our financial lives. We serve as goalies for ourselves and our families and without the help of good financial defenders such as health insurance, paycheck protection insurance, and life insurance we may find ourselves on the short end of an 8-0 financial score. Having a sound defense will also allow your financial scorers such as liquid savings accounts and retirement savings accounts to play more effectively in that there will be less pressure to score big. As you recruit your financial team, seek out a coach who can set up a good defense for you and your family. It will be one strategy move you will never regret.

SAMUEL M. DENNY

THE NET COST OF COLLEGE

As my wife and I were raising our children, one of our concerns was how we were going to pay for the cost of college. What at times froze us (and many families) into inaction were the tuition amounts quoted to us and the fact that we made too much money to qualify for need-based financial aid. But as the time approached for my daughter to start college, we were afforded some unexpected financial blessings that allowed us to educate both of our children without incurring debt. My daughter was now planning to attend a private college that at the time had an annual cost of about $22,000 per year. But even with the unexpected good fortune financially, I was still a bit overwhelmed as to how the cost of college would be handled. Then it occurred to me that there were additional changes in our financial situation that I had failed to take into account. What I determined was that there was a difference between the COST of college and the ADDITION-AL MONEY our family would be putting out.

My daughter would no longer be taking private dance lessons that had cost about $200 per month. She would no longer be participating in out-of-town dance competitions which on average had run around another $100 per month. Because she had done well academically in high school and continued to do so in college she was awarded about $6000 per year in scholarship money. Money she earned during her college years working part-time as a nurse's aide at a local hospital also helped with college costs. Finally, by virtue of her no longer living at home during the school year she would not be eating or sleeping at our home on a regular basis. Though I was not able to put a dollar figure on the savings, I did notice a difference in the food bill and the time it took to do the family laundry.

While the actual cost of my daughter's education was still $22,000, the additional cost to our family unit turned out to be less than half of that figure. The numbers will no doubt vary from situation to situation, yet the basic concept is the same. The college years are a time of change both financially and socially for many families. Being fully aware of those changes can only be to the benefit of parents and young people alike.

SAMUEL M. DENNY

ON REALIZING
"THE AMERICAN DREAM"

During its lengthy run on television, the Oprah Winfrey Show attracted a large following of persons from all walks of life. My wife was a regular viewer and on occasion I would watch as well. One of the regular guests on the Oprah Winfrey Show was financial advisor Suze Orman. During one of Suze Orman's appearances there was also a younger woman on stage who was relating to the audience how she had fallen into deep financial distress. A single parent with a twelve-year-old son, the woman had purchased a home a few years before and was now on the verge of losing it due to the structure of the mortgage loan. As the woman told her story, as a viewer I could see a person with the weight of the world on her shoulders. Repeatedly the statement was made that "I was getting the American Dream" as the result of buying a home. Desperate, the woman then asked Suze Orman for guidance that would enable her to keep the home she had purchased.

Suze Orman responded in a way that put the woman's emotional welfare ahead of her being able to remain in her home. The woman was told that the most important issue was not that she retain her home. To the contrary, the home needed to be sold and from there the woman and her son needed to move into an apartment that they could afford. The "American Dream" was that mother and son take a challenging situation and together make it workable and ultimately an opportunity to build character and values. Home first and foremost was a family unit of mother and son as opposed to a building.

Almost immediately I watched the woman's body language change from burdened to a sense of relief. Perhaps she would be no longer a homeowner, but she was no longer held prisoner by a value system dictated by outside sources. And when we as individuals feel the need to seek out financial counsel, we should take into consideration how valid the numerous outside messages we absorb on a regular basis are in our daily lives. Having financial resources is one thing. Having a healthy relationship with your resources is what will provide tranquility to your personal and your financial life.

SAMUEL M. DENNY

TO A "BAD BOY"—WITH RESPECT

During my years at Seneca High School I was a member of the largest graduating class the school has ever produced. As such there were a number of classmates who I never crossed paths with due to differences in academic course work, differences in outside interests, or both. One of those people was Tom Bush, who I only got to know in late 2012 while attending a class gathering at a Louisville restaurant. Up to that time I was aware of Tom only by reputation. In his own words, he was a "bad boy" who was more interested in fast cars and socializing than in the academic side of school life. Yet as Tom interacted with the group at large it became apparent that this was an intelligent, well-spoken man who cared about people from all walks of life. As it turned out, both Tom and I had a mutual interest in maintaining ties with our classmates. As such we exchanged phone numbers and agreed to stay in touch.

Over the next several months Tom and I had a number of phone conversations. As we talked I was taken as to how much we had in common. It seemed that we had utilized comparable skills in our working lives— Tom as a union steward and mine in financial services. Our values as to what we looked toward in life also turned out to be quite similar. And I knew I had a valued friend when one day my computer was hacked with a scam message stating that my wife Linda and I were stranded overseas and needed money. That night I received a call from Tom. Though he fully realized the E-mail was a bogus message, he still was concerned and was checking to see if we were OK. Relationships were important to Tom. The length of a friendship or how it had evolved was never an issue.

As our 45th high school reunion drew near Tom Bush became an integral part of the planning process. He worked to set up arrangements with a local restaurant for an informal gathering, helped to decorate the outdoor pavilion there, and the day of the event welcomed each of us as we arrived. After the reunion, Tom continued to work keeping classmates updated and helping to plan future class events. And on Labor Day weekend, 2016 Tom left home headed for a class gathering prepared to assist with grilling hamburgers for all in attendance.

Tom Bush never arrived at his destination. On the way there, he was involved in a head-on collision with a drunk driver and was killed instantly. Our group of over 30 learned of Tom's death while the get-together was in progress. All of us in attendance were in shock as to the news. What made this all the more overwhelming was that Tom Bush, a man who loved cars and loved people, was traveling in his most recently acquired vehicle to be with a group of friends he cared deeply about. He had died doing the things he most wanted to do, but knowing that did not made his passing any easier to process.

Each year when the Seneca High School yearbook was issued it was customary for students to get their friends to sign on one of the pages. Usually an additional message would accompany the signature. As Tom Bush and I did not cross paths during our high school years, neither of us would have had an opportunity to sign the other's yearbook. Given the opportunity to sign Tom Bush's Seneca High School yearbook today, my message would be one that hopefully would describe our short but fulfilling friendship. What I would write to Tom would be simply this:

"To a 'bad boy'—— with respect.

NOVEMBER 22, 1963
(A RECONNECTION)

Virtually all of us growing up during the 1960's remember the events surrounding the assassination of President John F. Kennedy and how we were affected personally. And those of us attending Seneca High School at that time can surely recall what class we were in that Friday afternoon when the news of the president's passing was announced over the intercom. In my case I was in a seventh-grade general art class taught by Mrs. Elsie Middleton. As for two of my high school classmates, Ed Henson and Greg Stairs, they were sitting beside each other in a junior high core class taught by Mrs. Mae Johnson. Ed recalls that at that moment Greg tried to verbalize some thoughts as to what had transpired, but was told immediately by the teacher that it simply was not the right time to do so.

As they progressed through junior high and later high school, Ed Henson and Greg Stairs became close friends. In addition to having the same classes they played junior varsity baseball together, ran cross country together, and did things together socially. Upon graduation in 1969 the two friends went their separate ways in part due to attending different colleges and in part due to Greg's family moving to New Jersey a couple of years afterward. It was not until 30 years later in 1999 that the two friends were able to reconnect at our class reunion. Ed had remained in Louisville working as a media broker and radio station owner. Greg, on the other hand, was now living in Dallas, TX and working as a partner in a software business. Once reconnected, the two friends continued to stay in touch. And in 2006 Ed was to be in the Dallas area on business and got in contact with Greg, arranging a time that they could get together and catch up.

The two friends had an enjoyable time together. They first attended a Texas Rangers baseball game accompanied by Greg's son and a business colleague of Ed's. Then after the game there was an additional reconnection that took both men back to the events of November 22, 1963. Prior to taking Ed and his colleague back to their hotel room, Greg drove down the route the Kennedy motorcade had taken that fateful day. The group saw the spot where the president had been shot. They saw the warehouse from where the shots were allegedly fired. And they were taken along the route leading to Parkland Memorial Hospital, where the president was taken for treatment prior to his death. The guided tour that Greg provided that night was an opportunity for both men (and Ed in particular) to reflect on an event that shaped the lives of all Americans. And in addition, the visit reaffirmed a friendship that had begun years before during junior high school.

As the 50th anniversary of the Kennedy assassination approaches, perhaps all of us should step back and take stock as to how the events in our lives affect us. Sometimes those events may be on a national stage as the Kennedy assassination was. Sometimes those events are simply taking the time to reconnect with long lost friends. Ed Henson and Greg Stairs continue to stay in contact, having again gotten together in Dallas last year. And just like these two friends, we all should be appreciative of the people and the opportunities that have been provided to each of us.

As appeared in the Louisville Courier-Journal (10-19-2013)

SAMUEL M. DENNY

"GOD BE WITH YOU IN YOUR LOSS"

Early in my working life, I was assigned to a position that I was not fully capable of handling competently. Though I had the formal education that the job required I did not as yet have the wisdom or experience needed to be successful. Yet things were further complicated in that my immediate supervisor had created a work situation where to do my job well would have been difficult to impossible for anyone. Almost from the beginning my supervisor attempted to have me removed from my position. After less than a year I was laid off as part of an organizational reduction in force, my confidence shattered and not knowing what my career path would be from there.

With the full support of my wife I changed careers. Things were a bit rocky to start but after a time it became apparent that I was in a good long-term career setting. Yet even though things were on an upward path there was still something gnawing at me as to the prior work assignment. Simply put, I had not fully accepted responsibility as to my shortcomings in the prior job and had not reached full closure as to that. An answer came to me one Sunday following a church service while reading a book in the church library. The author was stressing the importance of making amends as to your shortcomings and the emotional freedom that comes with such an action. I reflected on what I had read for several days. Finally, I sat down and did one of the hardest things I have ever done in my life. I wrote a letter of amends to my former supervisor.

I remember shaking both as I wrote the letter and later when I took it to be mailed. Yet at the same time I found I had gained the freedom to move completely forward in my life. At times I would wonder as to how my letter had been received. And there was something else that I sometimes wondered about but did not stress over. That was whether my former supervisor had any thoughts and feelings as to her role in what had been a toxic situation.

Early in 2012, my mother passed away due to heart failure. As my mother was well thought of by many people I received a number of sympathy cards. One day while checking the mail I noticed a card from a completely unexpected person. That person was my former supervisor, who did not know my mother or the family personally. The card was entitled "God Be With You In Your Loss" and included the following handwritten message:

"That which brings us sadness had once brought us joy. Cherish all that was yours. Your faith, family, and friends will certainly help to sustain you. Peace."

I had no doubts as to the sincerity of what had been written. I could not say what may have transpired after over 30 years to prompt the card being sent, but that didn't matter. And I also realized that a higher power had been with me years before as I grieved the loss of a career and did not know where to turn. The message in the card said it all. For during that time as well my faith, family, and friends had been there to fully sustain me.

My former supervisor died later in the year at the age of 88. In reading the obituary it appeared that this had been on the whole a life well lived. The message I would share with her family is the message sent to me earlier, which covers so much of what life throws at us:

"That which brings us sadness had once brought us joy. Cherish all that was yours. Your faith, family, and friends will certainly help to sustain you. Peace"

SAMUEL M. DENNY

ON FINANCIAL SERENITY

My wife and I participated in a family focus support group for several years. During that time, we both learned a number of things about ourselves and also about the counseling process itself. We learned that many times a surface behavior is but a symptom of a deeper issue that needs to be fully addressed. We also learned that the primary goal for each of us is not to effect change in the behavior of those around us, but instead to take steps to change our own behavior to allow us to relate to others in a healthier manner. More than once members of the group told stories of throwing money at a particular problem, only to find that the problem is worse than before. It seems that only stepping back and allowing those we love to "stand on their own two feet" do things begin to improve.

At the close of each session the group gathered, held hands, and repeated the Serenity Prayer of the Christian faith. It goes as follows:

"Grant me the serenity to accept the things I cannot change, the courage to change the things that I can, and the wisdom to know the difference. Just for today."

In our financial lives it seems the last thing the world at large desires for us as individuals is serenity. The messages that are sent to us on a daily basis by the news media (be it network television, the Internet, or the print media) seem to focus far more on the health of our national economy as opposed to any person within the economy. There is so much information and analysis out there that it often serves to cause us stress and paralyze us into inaction. Added to that is the blitz of commercial messages we process on a daily basis. The commercial messages may indeed be relevant to our situation, but even if we choose to act on those messages we often can never be completely sure that we have made a good decision.

How can financial serenity be attained? Perhaps just as is done in the counseling process, one must first determine the deeper issues that should be addressed and then work to make changes in financial behavior. We have little control over the fiscal policy of our government or the world at large. What we can control is our approach toward our individual financial situation. We can stay informed on financial issues, yet also realize that information and knowledge are not necessarily the same thing. We can provide for our families, yet also be aware that we do not have to succumb to every commercial message we hear. We can also be appreciative of the many advantages each of us has been provided with, a point that can be driven home simply by experiencing a power outage at your residence for a period of time. And just as in one's personal life we can apply the Serenity message to our financial lives as well:

"Grant me the serenity to accept the things I cannot change, the courage to change the things that I can, and the wisdom to know the difference. Just for today."

THE INVESTMENT OF A LIFETIME

The most memorable expressions of love are not always frilly cards with store-bought verses, or heart-shaped boxes of chocolates. Often they are no more than a momentary glance that voices a silent "I love you." Or thoughts straight from the heart that—though imprinted on plain paper with the worn keys of an old typewriter in 1959—remain a treasure for the person for whom they are written. Such was the last letter my father passed on to my mother. My mother found the message in an envelope marked, "To be opened in the event of my death" after my father died in early 1997. My mother cried upon reading his words:

Memo to Patricia W. Denny—December 16, 1959

Pat, if you ever have occasion to read this perhaps you will think that I want to think for you even after I am gone. There are many things I would like to say as I sit at the office typing this memo. Some of the things I wish to cover are things I have thought about for a long time and have never gotten around to putting in writing.

I do not say this to make you sad, but to make you feel better. I have always loved you. With my perfectionist type personality and short temper I feel that I have never been capable of giving you the love to which you are entitled. Again, I say I have loved you and been proud of you as a wife and as a mother.

. . . Once I am gone I want my memory to hold no strings on you. I would of course want you to remember me as a happy part of your past, but not as a sad part of your future. What I am trying to say is this, lead a normal life—if a guy worthy of you comes along—marry him. If you get an opportunity to enjoy life in some other way don't be bound by tradition. Remember this, the past was fun and a wonderful part of your life, but it is the past. . . Even if we had no children I would feel the way I have stated above, but with children it is all the more important. They should see you as you are capable of being—enjoy them and enjoy life.

Love, W.S.

GOING MY WAY

I would like to think that there was a higher power looking over my father's shoulder the day he wrote these words to my mother. Yet what gave the words their depth and meaning was that they were totally consistent with the way my father conducted himself in marriage. He had invested wisely in my mother (and my mother in him) over a period of 47 ½ years. And my mother as a widow continued to live her life to the fullest. At 67 years of age she went on a mission trip to Cuba and from there found her calling ministering to the Hispanic community. She found a gentleman companion who was a man of character and compassion. Though they did not marry, they enjoyed a close relationship for a number of years. Friendships that were formed during the marriage did not die, but continued in a slightly different form. And a number of new friendships were formed, serving to enrich my mother's life all the more.

I was once told that when a loved one dies "time has a way of alleviating the sorrow, but not the missing." Yet in one respect if we have invested wisely in our relationships, there is a part of us that will always remain with our loved ones. My father had a sense of that on that winter day in 1959 as he wrote to my mother, not knowing when and under what set of circumstances my mother would read his message. And what better legacy can one leave behind than this—a message of love and affirmation towards those whose lives we have touched.

SAMUEL M. DENNY

"GO TO HELL"—A STORY OF LIFELONG (AND BEYOND) FRIENDSHIP

Toward the end of my father's life I came over to visit him while my mother was out with friends. During my visit my father received a telephone call and upon determining who was calling immediately said in a strong tone of voice "GO TO HELL." I was shocked as to what I had just heard my father say. Yet what shocked me even more was that he seemed to be having a pleasant conversation with the other person. After a good bit of time the conversation ended and at that point I asked my father "Dad, who did you just tell to 'go to hell?' You never would have had me talk to anyone like that." Upon hearing his answer I understood completely. He simply said "Chuck."

Chuck was Chuck Keiser, my father's best friend. Their friendship began during their college days and continued for over 50 years. My mother and Chuck's wife Betty Ann also became close friends. Our families visited back and forth regularly and I found it refreshing to compare Chuck's small town life in Eminence, Kentucky to the metropolitan life I experienced growing up in Louisville. And when either Chuck or my father got in contact with the other their standard greeting was 'GO TO HELL.' And many a time one of Chuck's sons was around while Chuck was extending the standard greeting to my father.

My father passed away in 1997 and Chuck died five years later in 2002. Though like all of us I have no idea as to what the hereafter is like I would like to envision how things might have been when Chuck was on his way up and my father saw him coming. For as with all close friends who have not seen each other in a while my father was excited to see Chuck.

You know how my father greeted Chuck.

And you know how Chuck greeted my father.

Suddenly a loud and booming voice was heard and both men came to attention. The diety in charge had a matter to take up with them. "Fellas, we need to have a talk," the diety began. "I hope you know how you got here. Both of you led honorable lives while on earth. You married good women and took care of them. You raised your children with a strong set of values. You worked hard to provide for your families. And you were the kind of friend anyone would have wanted to have."

'BUT DAMN IT, YOU TWO NEED TO WATCH YOUR LANGUAGE. SOMEONE AROUND HERE JUST MIGHT TAKE YOU SERIOUSLY.'

EPILOGUE—
"LIFETIME COACH"

When I was 12 and my brother was 9, our father was our Little League baseball coach. I treasure that experience for a number of reasons, even beyond the fact that our team, after a slow start, finished as league champion. My father used the baseball diamond to teach all of us life lessons as to giving your best effort, being alert and aware, and staying positive and supportive towards others. I knew my father to be an outstanding youth sports coach—I was told that by a number of people. After that memorable season, I was determined to follow in his footsteps as a youth sports coach.

Beginning at age 13, I spent five seasons as a volunteer coaching tee ball at a large metropolitan Little League baseball program. From there I coached older players in the same Little League program for seven seasons (with some time taken off when I became a parent).

Yet the majority of my coaching activity took place in an unexpected setting. That was as a volunteer youth soccer coach for 4 and 5 year olds at the local YMCA.

I began coaching soccer when my son was 5. I had never played the game and was not sure whether there was much I could teach young players. I soon learned that beyond being encouraging and enthusiastic, I only needed to pass on two basic concepts to the players—which way they were to go on the field and where the restroom facilities were. Over time, I found I loved the structure the game of soccer could provide for children of such a young age. Even after my son got older, I continued coaching at this age level, leaving after 20 years only because I had responsibilities for aging parents.

At age 60, I thought my coaching career was over. Yet when my grandson came of an age to play organized sports, I found myself called on again to coach. This time my fellow coaches were my son and daughter.

GOING MY WAY

I anticipated coaching my grandson until he moved on to the next age level. From there I envisioned myself fully retired from coaching.

My grandson's final season started uneventfully, but around the middle of the season, I became ill and was hospitalized for emergency abdominal surgery. I was unable to finish the season with the team as coach but was present for the team's final game. The day of the last game I watched from the team bench and observed my son and daughter as they were passing on the lessons of effort, awareness, and support to each child. After the game was over, awards were presented to each team member. Yet it was the final award presented that touched me at the core of my being.

My son got up and in front of the team and the parents presented me with a "Lifetime Coach" award. I was given an engraved jewelry box and a soccer ball with a touching message from my daughter written on it. The gesture brought me completely to tears. What greater tribute can parents be given by their children than being told in front of others that they have been an inspirational role model? I left the field that day completely overwhelmed with emotion. As I told both of my children "it has been a great ride." And it was a ride that had begun over 50 years before—starting and ending with valuable life's lessons being passed on from parent to child.

I have often wondered what it would have been like to have coached with my father. My father became disabled only two years after that special baseball season and as such was no longer able to coach youth sports. Yet in a way my father never stopped coaching. Despite his physical limitations, he never stopped giving his best effort whether as husband, father, or friend. As parents, all of us are life coaches for our children. The instruction does not always occur on an athletic field. The awards are not always a championship trophy. But when the payoff for one's efforts is being told in front of others that you have been an inspiration to those you have encountered how can you not walk away a winner? May each of you have such a moment of honor over the course of your lifetime.

– Sam Denny

www.ingramcontent.com/pod-product-compliance
Lightning Source LLC
Chambersburg PA
CBHW022111210326
41521CB00028B/310